ASA Special Series No. 36

Advocacy in International Commercial Arbitration

Elliott Geisinger
Guillaume Tattevin

Editors

Association Suisse de l'Arbitrage
Schweiz. Vereinigung für Schiedsgerichtsbarkeit
Associazione Svizzera per l'Arbitrato
Swiss Arbitration Association

JURIS

Questions About This Publication

For assistance with shipments, billing or other customer service matters, please call our Customer Services Department at:

1-631-350-2100

To obtain a copy of this book, call our Sales Department:

1-631-351-5430
Fax: 1-631-351-5712

Toll Free Order Line:

1-800-887-4064 (United States and Canada)

See our web page about this book:
www.arbitrationlaw.com

Printed in the United States of America
ISBN 978-1-933833-91-0

JurisNet, LLC
71 New Street
Huntington, New York 11743
USA
www.arbitrationlaw.com

TABLE OF CONTENTS

FOREWORD

It is often said that no arbitration is any better than the arbitrator or arbitrators who are in charge. There is much truth to this proposition. It is, however, incomplete. For example, the parties also have a significant role to play in the process, and have important responsibilities of their own in this respect. That said, it is difficult to overestimate the role of counsel in determining the architecture of arbitral proceedings, in ensuring that the proceedings unfold efficiently and fairly and in acting as an essential bridge between their clients and the arbitral tribunal. Just as much as the arbitrators, counsel deserve credit for efficient proceedings - and blame for waste of time and money. This places significant responsibilities on counsel, not only for each individual case, but also for the long-term legitimacy of the arbitral process.

It is thus an essential role of any institution that seeks to promote arbitration as an ever-increasingly accepted means of dispute resolution to seek to foster the development of efficient advocacy in arbitration. The Swiss Arbitration Association ("ASA"), being an internationally recognised forum dedicated to the promotion of arbitration that is at the same time based in a crossroads of arbitration practices, is thus ideally placed to bring its contribution to what must be a continuous global effort.

On 29 January 2010, ASA organized a conference in Geneva on "Advocacy in International Arbitration". The goal of this conference was to launch and promote the newly created ASA Charter for Advocacy in International Commercial Arbitration, which seeks to identify, on a flexible and ever-evolving basis, best practices that make arbitration what it should be. When creating the ASA Charter, ASA was not claiming to have discovered the Philosopher's Stone of international arbitration: the ASA Charter sets out basic and widely-recognised principles for international arbitration advocates.

To enhance the visibility of these best practices and to recognize achievements in that field, ASA also decided to create a prize, the ASA Prize for Advocacy in International Commercial Arbitration. The goal of the ASA Prize is to provide recognition to counsel who, through their exceptional talents in advocacy, contribute most effectively to the promotion of effective resolution of international commercial disputes through arbitration. The first ASA Prize was awarded at the conference of 29 January 2010. The ASA Prize was awarded a second time in January 2012.

This volume of the ASA Special Series is a continuation of ASA's efforts in identifying and promoting efficient advocacy in international arbitration. To better explain the contents of the various contributions, it is necessary to take a step back and to consider a few realities, trends and needs.

Whilst in the courts, advocacy work is often constrained—or at the very least strongly impregnated—by strict rules of civil procedure and long-accepted practices, the reverse is true in arbitration: it is the parties, and more significantly counsel who have largely shaped arbitration as it is today. There is no reason to believe that the huge influence of counsel will diminish in coming years.

Along with this huge influence must come great responsibility. If arbitration is to continue to be accepted as the preferred means of dispute resolution in international commerce, it must be not only fair but also viable in terms of costs and time to decision, and demonstrably so. The role of counsel is critical in this respect. Regrettably, the last two decades have seen counsel increasingly lose sight of this responsibility. There is a tendency to render complicated what is simple, to ape proceedings tailored for national court systems and, under the guise of a "melting point pot" of various legal traditions, to combine the worst and leave aside the best of what these traditions have to offer.

When this point is made to arbitration practitioners, quite a few will argue that their primary duties are to their clients rather than to arbitration. To paraphrase an oft-quoted statesman: they do not have arbitration's telephone number, whereas their clients very much know how to reach them.

Fortunately, advocacy is an area where any improvement will directly serve clients as well as the arbitral process as a whole. The principle that counsel should strive for better advocacy is therefore not controversial—it is the theoretical definition and practical implementation of "efficient" advocacy that remain elusive. Hence the ASA Charter, which should be seen as part of the global effort to identify some basic and widely recognised principles that define "efficient" advocacy in arbitration. Whether these principles are as widely observed as they are recognised is another question. Elliott Geisinger's contribution explores this issue in a deliberately provocative tone, and warns of the dangers lying beneath the surface of what many consider to be "best" practices.

Moreover, in recognition of the trends and needs described above, recent years have seen the rise of institutions and programmes offering advocacy training to professionals, as well as arbitration competitions for students, some of which were presented at the ASA Conference on 29 January 2010 and are set out in this volume, particularly in Professor Waincymer's enlightened contributions on the training of advocates.

The selections of the initial ASA Prize laureate in 2010 and the second recipient in 2012 were eye-openers, both on the level of interest elicited by the ASA Prize and on the very diverse ways in which candidates were perceived as outstanding advocates. The lesson is that greatness in advocacy comes in many different ways. This confirmed ASA's position that the purpose of advocacy training is not to elicit the manufacture of advocacy-clones nor to rub away the differences between jurisdictions. Advocacy is shaped by the complex professional constraints in which counsel from various jurisdictions evolve, as Matt Gearing and Sheila Ahuja make clear in this volume.

ASA's goal in coming years will be to press towards the goals set by the ASA Charter by all possible means. ASA will strive to enhance advocacy while ensuring that arbitration retains the diversity that makes its strength. Future evolutions of the ASA Charter and future recipients of the ASA Prize will hopefully testify to ASA's success.

Elliott Geisinger
Guillaume Tattevin

ABOUT THE EDITORS

Elliott Geisinger is a Partner in the International Arbitration Group of Schellenberg Wittmer in Geneva. Since 1994, his practice has focused on international arbitration. He has acted as counsel and arbitrator in complex commercial disputes involving international construction contracts, consortia and joint venture agreements, sponsorship contracts, sales and distribution contracts, and consultancy contracts while also advising clients in investment matters.

In addition, Mr. Geisinger has regularly represented clients in arbitration-related court proceedings, and several of his cases have been reported on in the official collection of Swiss Supreme Court cases and in arbitration journals. Contract management in large scale construction projects is a further specialization of his. He has also advised Swiss corporations in investment disputes.

After graduating from the School of Law of the University of Geneva in 1986, where he also obtained a Master of Laws in 1990, Mr. Geisinger served as a teaching and research assistant in private international law at the university from 1986 to 1992. He was a trainee and then an Associate with Baker & McKenzie in Geneva before joining Schellenberg Wittmer in 1996 and becoming a Partner in 2002. He sat on the Arbitration Committee of the Geneva Chamber of Commerce and Industry from 1999 to 2003 and was elected to the executive board of the Swiss Arbitration Association in 2007, becoming Vice President in 2010. He has authored and co-authored several publications in the fields of international arbitration and private international law.

Guillaume Tattevin is a Senior Associate at LALIVE in Geneva, where he practices international arbitration. He has acted as Counsel, Arbitrator and Tribunal Secretary in numerous international arbitration proceedings, both *ad hoc* and institutional (including under the rules of the ICC, Swiss Chambers, UNCITRAL, CAS, NAI and PCA).

Before joining LALIVE, Mr. Tattevin worked as Legal Counsel at the Permanent Court of Arbitration in The Hague and as an Associate in the arbitration and litigation department of Freshfields Bruckhaus Deringer in Paris.

Mr. Tattevin qualified to practice law in Paris in 2003. He is a member of the Swiss Arbitration Association (ASA), ASA below 40, the section of foreign lawyers of the Geneva Bar Association, and the Paris Bar Association. He holds a D.E.A. in International Law from the University of Paris II Panthéon-Assas and an LL.M. in European Community Law from the University of Essex.

ABOUT THE AUTHORS

Sheila Ahuja is an Associate in Allen & Overy's Hong Kong office. She has been involved in a range of arbitrations involving various jurisdictions such as India, England and Wales and the Philippines. She has assisted in court and arbitration proceedings involving disputes relating to derivatives transactions and has also assisted international corporations in relation to regulatory investigations before disciplinary bodies in Hong Kong and England and Wales. Her recent experience includes representing an international oil and gas major and its Indian joint venture partner in arbitration proceedings commenced against the Government of India under the UNCITRAL Rules, representing a European construction and engineering company in an ICSID arbitration against the Government of Philippines, and representing a European investment bank in derivatives arbitration in London under the LCIA Rules.

Ms. Ahuja is admitted to practice in Hong Kong and England and Wales. She studied in London, Hong Kong and Cambridge.

Matthew Gearing is a Partner in Allen & Overy LLP in the Litigation Group, specialising in international arbitration. His experience includes arbitrations under the ICC, UNCITRAL, SIAC, HKIAC, SCC, LCIA and ICSID Rules in Europe, South America, Trinidad, Barbados, Tanzania, Pakistan, India, Sri Lanka, the former Soviet Union, the Philippines, the People's Republic of China, Korea, Singapore, Vietnam and Indonesia as well as Hong Kong. Mr. Gearing often appears as advocate in his cases. He is a past Co-Chair of the LCIA's Young International Arbitration Group, a member of the LCIA's Asia Pacific Users Council and a Council Member of the Hong Kong International Arbitration Centre. Mr. Gearing is a joint editor of "Russell on Arbitration" and has written and spoken widely on arbitration.

Mr. Gearing qualified in England in 1997, where he is now a Solicitor-Advocate, and qualified in Hong Kong in 2001. He has been based in both London and Hong Kong offices and has acted in a large number of complex and high profile arbitrations around the world.

Bernard Hanotiau is a member of the Brussels and Paris Bars. Since 1978, Mr. Hanotiau has been actively involved in more than 350 international arbitration cases as party-appointed Arbitrator, Chairman, Sole Arbitrator, Counsel and Expert in all parts of the world.

Mr. Hanotiau is a Professor at the law school of Louvain University (Belgium) where he teaches international arbitration. He is a member of the ICCA Council and of the Council of the ICC Institute and a member of the ICC International Arbitration Commission. He is also vice-President of the Institute of Transnational Arbitration (Dallas) and a former vice-President of the LCIA Court. He is a member of the Board of Advisors of the Singapore International Arbitration Center and of the International Advisory Board of the Hong Kong International Arbitration Centre.

He is the author of *Complex Arbitrations: Multiparty, Multicontract, Multi-issue and Class Actions* (Kluwer, 2006) and of more than 120 articles, most of them relating to international commercial law and arbitration. In March 2011, Mr. Hanotiau received the GAR "Arbitrator of the Year" award.

Henry Peter is Professor of Law at the University of Geneva. Since 1998 he has been Program Director of the Master in Business Law common to the Universities of Lausanne and Geneva. He is also a visiting professor at the University of Freiburg and the University of Lyon 3-Jean Moulin (under a program LL.M. in International and European Law).

Besides his teaching and research, Mr. Peter is Senior Partner in a law firm in Lugano. He is frequently appointed as presiding arbitrator, sole arbitrator or co-arbitrator in commercial or sports arbitration.

He has been a member of the Swiss Takeover Board since 2004 and of the Swiss Commission of sanctions on the Swiss Exchange since 2007. He was President of the Geneva Business Law Association from 2003 to 2006. He is a member of the editing board of the Swiss Review of business and financial market law and a board member of the Banking and finance law Centre at the University of Geneva. He is a vice-President of the Swiss Olympic Association chamber disciplinary panel for doping cases. Between 2003 and 2008, he was a member of the expert group on the *Concordat* insolvency proceedings appointed by the Swiss Federal Office of Justice. He is a member of the Swiss Arbitration Association and president of its Swiss Italian section since 2003.

Mr. Peter was honorary consul of Sweden for the Italian-speaking part of Switzerland from 1994 to 2010. He has authored or edited numerous books and articles in his various fields of activity.

Jeffrey Waincymer is an Arbitrator and Mediator and a Professor of international trade law at the faculty of law, Monash University in Melbourne, Australia. He teaches in the fields of arbitration, various international trade subjects, taxation and advocacy through the Vis Moot commercial arbitration competition. He has taught for over 25 years to undergraduates, post-graduates and also to Australian and foreign government officials. He is regularly invited to conduct training programs run through government and aid agencies.

Mr. Waincymer is a Qualified Legal Practitioner and Accredited Mediator, practicing solely in the fields of international trade, customs, arbitration and ADR. He is also an Australian Government Nominee as a panellist for the WTO and has acted as a panellist. He has been an Australian government nominated ICSID panellist, is on the arbitral panels of SIAC, HKIAC, ICDR and KLRCA as well as being a fellow of ACICA. He has also been a consultant to the Australian Law Reform Commission, the Administrative Review Council, the Victorian Government and a number of Federal Departments and agencies.

His research is primarily in the fields of international trade law, arbitration and taxation. He is the author of *Procedure and Evidence in International Arbitration* (Kluwer 2012); *WTO Litigation: Procedural Aspects of Formal Dispute Settlement*; *Australian Income Tax: Principles and Policy, Second Edition;* and a joint author of *A Practical Guide to International Commercial Arbitration;* and *International Trade Law: Commentary and Materials, Second Edition.*

PART I

Advocacy:
Which Qualities for Advocates?

Advocacy in International Commercial Arbitration: What For?

Elliott Geisinger[1]

1. INTRODUCTION

The question set out in the title of this contribution may appear provocative or nonsensical (or both). It was inspired by the famous case *Board of Inland Revenue v. Haddock*, "reported" in A. P. Herbert's "*Uncommon Law*",[2] the sub-title of which is "*Why is the House of Lords?*"—an unusual query, no doubt, but not an unreasonable one upon closer examination.[3]

Coming back to the topic of this article: Why indeed enquire as to the purpose of advocacy in international commercial arbitration when the answer appears to be obvious? The response is simple: the answer is not so obvious. Indeed, observation and experience show that the term "advocacy" can mean very different things depending on the standpoint one takes. Thus, it does not (or not necessarily) have the same meaning for clients, counsel and arbitrators. To add another layer of variables, "advocacy" can be understood very differently depending on whether one is East or West of Suez, North or South of the Equator or on this or that shore of the Atlantic.

---

1 Partner, Schellenberg Wittmer, Vice-Chair of ASA.

2 First published in 1935. Copyright © Teresa Elizabeth Perkins and Jocelyn Herbert. Reprinted *inter alia* in 2001 by House of Stratus. This is only one of the many "cases" opposing Mr. Albert Haddock and His (at the time) Majesty's taxmen.

3 Among the gems to be read (or re-read) from the speech of the Master of the Rolls in this "case":

> The human mind is admittedly fallible, and in most professions the possibility of occasional error is admitted and even guarded against. But the legal profession is the only one in which the chances of error are admitted to be so high that an elaborate machinery has been provided for the correction of error—not a single error, but a succession of errors. In other trades to be wrong is regarded as a matter for regret; in the law alone it is regarded as a matter of course. [...] To take a fair parallel, our great doctors, I think, would not claim to be more respected or more advanced in their own science than our greatest jurists. But our surprise would be great if, after the removal of our appendix by a distinguished surgeon, we were taken before three other distinguished surgeons, who ordered our appendix to be replaced; and our surprise would give place to stupefaction if we were then referred to a tribunal of seven distinguished surgeons, who directed that our appendix should be extracted again. Yet such operations, or succession of operations, are an everyday experience in the practice of the law.

This article does not purport to be an exhaustive analysis of the functions of advocacy in international arbitration, let alone a comparative digest of the various practices encountered across the globe. Its aim is far more humble: it takes as a starting point the guiding principles proposed in the "*ASA Charter of Advocacy in International Arbitration*" of the Swiss Arbitration Association (the "ASA Charter")[4], as well as contributions from panelists at ASA's Conference of 29 January 2010 on Advocacy in International Commercial Arbitration (the "ASA Conference"). It offers some thoughts on what "advocacy" means in the field of international commercial arbitration. It will then examine two examples—expert evidence and site visits—to illustrate the pitfalls of what one would consider to be "effective" advocacy.[5]

2. WHAT DOES "ADVOCACY" MEAN?

2.1. Terminology

Before delving into our subject, some terminological clarifications are necessary. Indeed, even among lawyers, the term "advocacy" can mean different things. This can lead to considerable confusion.

The 2010 edition of *Webster's New World Law Dictionary* defines the term "advocacy" as "Active support for a legal cause by argument and persuasion". Browsing through the Internet, one finds further examples: "Advocacy is the act of pleading for or arguing in favor of something or actively supporting a cause or proposal. It can also refer to the work or profession of an advocate. For lawyers advocacy means representing the interests of the client in the best manner possible. Advocacy is considered an art in which lawyers are trained".[6] Such broad definitions are relatively straightforward. They are familiar to practitioners, who immediately recognise this as a fair (if perhaps flattering) description of their work.

However, in certain jurisdictions, the term "advocacy" receives a far narrower definition. For example, the Oxford Dictionary gives a general definition that is very similar to those set out above, but also a second definition relating to the role of the legal profession in the courts: an "advocate" is "a professional pleader in a court of justice".

---

4 The text of the ASA Charter can be downloaded from ASA's website: www.arbitration-ch.org.

5 Another objective of this contribution will be achieved if the reader finds it at times thought-provoking. Finally, this contribution unabashedly aims to entertain the reader (hence the light tone and not always scientific footnoting).

6 This definition is taken from www.uslegal.com.

This narrow definition thus equates "advocacy" with oral interventions in hearings (for example: examination of witnesses; giving oral argument; answering questions from the bench), as opposed to the gathering of the evidence and similar groundwork of the case in direct contact with the client. Counsel trained in Civil Law jurisdiction will generally handle both roles, which are subsumed in the role of the "avocat". In this sense, the words "advocate" and "avocat" are false friends. Hence the great potential for speaking at cross-purposes when one side of a conversation says "advocacy" having in mind the narrow definition and the other understands "advocacy" to cover the broad concept.[7] For that matter, this occurred on (rare) occasions during the ASA Conference.

Like the ASA Charter, this contribution will use the term "advocacy" in the broader sense. It covers the role of counsel in international arbitration, from the first case analyses to the closing submissions (be they oral or written).

2.2. Is There a "One-Size-Fits-All" Standard of "Good" Advocacy?

Having defined advocacy, we now move to what could be recognised as being "good" advocacy. The reader of the ASA Charter will understand that "good" advocacy has a broadly accepted meaning in international commercial arbitration: presenting a party's case to the arbitral tribunal in such a manner as to maximise that party's chances of winning its case in a cost- and time-efficient manner. This is hardly surprising and will indeed be the case generally. However, things are more subtle than they seem.

2.2.1. "Good" advocacy seen from the client's perspective

A first (and not at all obvious) question is the role that clients expect counsel to take. An intervention at the ASA Conference by Mr. Bruce Gailey, then Chief Litigation Counsel at Alstom Power, put the question perfectly. He said that he was unhappy whenever outside counsel would say that a given case was "his" or "her" case. For this highly sophisticated user of international commercial arbitration, counsel should never forget who "owns" the case: the client. This has important consequences in terms of case management for the advocate, since he or she must take care not only to keep the client's objectives in

[7] A good example is the puzzlement sometimes experienced by Civil Law-trained practitioners when a Common Law-trained colleague asks: "Who will be doing the advocacy?"

mind at all times, but also to inform the client fully on all aspects of the case that the "case owner" will want to know. In other words, this means that the client will be heavily involved at all stages of the proceedings.

The idea that the client "owns" the case is of course perfectly desirable. It is sometimes difficult to implement, at least in the early stages of the relationship with counsel. For example, whilst clients wish to be informed and involved, they are also busy people who do not want to receive superfluous and non-essential emails or telephone calls. It is therefore necessary to strike a balance, and this can involve a trial-and-error learning phase. Moreover, even once a proper balance is struck, significant client involvement is generally synonymous with higher legal fees because of the additional time that a high degree of client involvement entails. There is nothing wrong with this as such, provided that the client and its counsel are aware of this factor and (both) accept it. By contrast, some clients actually want their outside counsel to take over the case and require only minimal interaction and sometimes even only minimal reporting (although such clients are increasingly rare). It is not always easy for counsel to identify which profile a given new client has in this respect.

In addition, and this is an important comment in the field of international arbitration, the cultural and legal background of the client and of counsel will strongly influence the degree in which they will consider the client's involvement to be necessary or appropriate. When asked, during the preparation of the ASA Conference, whether he had noted on this subject differences in approach depending on the cultural and legal background of the client or of counsel, Mr. Gailey answered, "Definitely—ranging from lawyers who are almost passive and virtually let the client run the case to those who would—if they could—take instructions at the outset and inform the client of the result at the end. I have spoken with lawyers in at least three jurisdictions who referred to a case as "my case"—and resented the client taking an active role. I think there is a large cultural component to this".

Second, clients of course want to win the case, but at what cost? This is an absolutely essential feature of good advocacy. It means that the advocate must explain to the client the various options that are open in approaching the case: will it be a full-scale "leave-no-stone-unturned" case, or do the client's strategic needs (or, for that matter, financial capacities) require "leaner" case management? Failure to address this crucial question at the outset is a very dangerous mistake. Counsel may believe that the client wishes him or her to explore all legal and factual avenues, whilst the client may have understood that the role of counsel was to present a "bare bones" case (or vice-versa). If this type of misunderstanding arises, there will be a very serious difference in opinion as to whether counsel's work qualifies as "good advocacy".

A third (and related) question is time: the client wants to win, but when? Is counsel expected to complete the case quickly, or is the client prepared to "take whatever time it takes"? This, again, is a crucial issue, for it will contribute to determine the case strategy: if speed is given priority, this can mean renouncing certain forms of evidence (in particular expert evidence) and, more generally, limiting the time that is at the advocate's disposal fully to investigate the facts. In other words, giving speed the priority can mean a trade-off against the chances of success. This is a particularly difficult factor to manage because at the start of the proceedings, counsel can only rarely determine with any certainty the actual complexity of a case; and the opponent's behaviour—a major potential source of delay—is practically impossible to predict accurately.

A fourth question that will determine the performance of an advocate in the client's eyes will be the client's willingness to be forthcoming with the facts, especially facts that are adverse to the client's case (for example the contractor in a design-build construction contract whose engineering department failed to provide adequate design), or facts that are potentially adverse to the client's overall business interests (for example behaviour that is questionable from the perspective of competition law). Counsel cannot discharge their fundamental duties if the client holds back important information, if the client reacts badly when faced with critical examination of its performance or if the client resents what it perceives to be prying questions. Yet, the ASA Charter states that it is counsel's duty to inform the client clearly and candidly about the strengths and the weaknesses of the case. Again, the assessment of the quality of counsel's work may be very different depending on whether it is viewed from the client's or counsel's perspective.

The cultural factor plays an especially important role in this respect. The author of this contribution learned "the hard way" that an objective and cold appraisal of a client's case, in particular the weaknesses of the case, may well be a matter of course in certain parts of the world, but that an explanation of the client's strengths and weaknesses requires a powerful dose of diplomacy in others. What clients in some parts of the world would consider to be a minimum standard of good advocacy could qualify elsewhere as a lack of supportiveness (if not as being downright insulting).

Fifth and finally, it is necessary to determine whether the client actually wants to win the arbitration in the first place, and whether this goal should be achieved quickly and cost-efficiently. Indeed, "success" can be defined in many ways:

- As respondent, a party may be resigned to losing the case, but will consider itself to be "successful" if it delays that outcome.[8]
- As claimant, a party may make tactical claims aimed at attracting the attention of the opponent's management in view of settlement (an admittedly dangerous course of action).
- Claimants may also initiate proceedings with the aim of sending a message to the market that they will not tolerate certain forms of behaviour. Whether they actually prevail on the merits can be of secondary importance in such cases.
- In extreme cases, the strategic purpose of the arbitration is the arbitration itself: parties sometimes bring tactical or even vexatious claims aimed at destroying the opposite party through protracted and costly procedures. In this case, the longer the proceedings last and the more they cost, the more "successful" one party will consider itself to be. It is hoped that such cases are rare.
- Finally, even if a party wants to win, it may also knowingly adopt tactics that will make this result more expensive and delay the outcome of the proceedings. One particularly egregious example of this approach is when a party knows that its opponent has retained counsel on a capped-fee basis. This will frequently be common knowledge where the opposite party is a State or a State-controlled entity and has sent tenders to law firms seeking bids. If a party knows that its opponent's lawyers will be paid only up to a pre-defined cap, it may decide to multiply procedural motions and requests for evidence-taking, in the knowledge that this will

---

[8] This is not necessarily illegitimate. For example, a defence against an opposite party seeking declaratory relief that it validly terminated a contract for cause can be "successful" even if such relief is ultimately granted, but only after the respondent made in the meantime a successful bid in a tender that would otherwise have required flagging any contracts that were found to have been terminated for cause. Similarly, cash-flow problems can justify a guerrilla-type defence against a monetary claim if the claimant is unwilling to accept reasonable instalments.

result in the opposite party's counsel reaching the cap quickly. Most regrettably, this strategy pays off when it leads the opponent's senior counsel to disengage from the case and delegate more and more work to inexperienced juniors. Such tactics may elicit moral opprobrium (and arbitrators can sanction such behaviour in their rulings on costs), but the fact remains that this is how some parties and counsel operate. From their perspective, what some would consider abhorrent qualifies as "good" advocacy.

2.2.2. "Good" advocacy seen from the perspective of arbitrators

Whilst practically all arbitrators will agree that a "good" advocate is someone who makes their work as easy as possible—by which the author means making it as easy as possible to render an award based on a good understanding of the factual and legal issues of the case—arbitrators will also have varying views on what is "good" advocacy.

Arbitrators' own legal and cultural background will strongly influence their perceptions in this regard. This raises an important issue: arbitrators must have the openness of mind to understand the different cultural and legal background of the parties before them and of their counsel.

For example, an arbitrator who is at the same time a US trial attorney or an English Barrister might be aghast at the number of open questions (even the dread "*Why?*") that lawyers from Civil Law jurisdictions tend to put to witnesses—whilst their continental colleagues will see this as a way of getting to the facts faster than with controlled and closed questions. Conversely, arbitrators trained in Civil Law jurisdictions will often experience a sharp drop in their enthusiasm when counsel addresses a witness with an "I put it to you that..."—whilst many of their Common Law-trained colleagues will perceive this to be a matter of simple fairness to the witness. Neither is right or wrong.

In this connection, there is a trend towards "standardisation" of procedures in international arbitration, in particular techniques for advocacy. This is welcome to the extent that it mitigates the risk of misunderstandings. However, it is a matter of life experience that "standardisation" is frequently concomitant with a closing of the mind to whatever falls outside the "standard". In other words, "standardisation" can never relieve arbitrators from their duty to grasp the cultural and legal background of counsel appearing before them.

Thus, being well-versed in "standard" procedures does not necessarily equate with being an "effective" advocate.

2.2.3. "Good" advocacy seen from the perspective of counsel

One of Honoré Daumier's more hilarious prints is *Maître Chapotard lisant dans un journal judiciaire l'éloge de lui-même par lui-même,* depicting an evidently self-satisfied advocate reading in a legal gazette an article praising him, and written by him. As with all of Daumier's works, there is more than a little truth here: lawyers are generally not known to be the most self-critical profession in the world. Reverting to the subject of this contribution, this remark needs to be put into context by citing a few key passages of the ASA Charter.

Regarding "the principal objective of international commercial arbitration", the ASA Charter states that it "must be the efficiency of the process, avoiding unnecessary confrontation, producing fair and equitable results and contributing to the restoration of constructive business relations". Another key exhortation in the ASA Charter reads as follow: "When approaching international arbitration proceedings, Counsel should be mindful that the training and experience of other players in the process may differ, having regard to various legal, social and cultural backgrounds". Other important passages of the ASA Charter remind counsel that the "the purpose of the procedure is to resolve the dispute and not to settle personal scores between the protagonists. Counsel should contribute to a sober and business-like approach to the procedure" and "personal attacks should be avoided".

This translates into the following cardinal principles governing the relation between counsel and the arbitral tribunal:

> Effective advocacy in international commercial arbitration is above all communication with the tribunal, understanding its task and assisting the tribunal in meeting its obligations. This implies the following:
>
> - making a clear, concise and user-friendly presentation of the case, setting out the position of the party represented by Counsel and identifying those aspects in which this position differs from that of the opponent(s);
> - ensuring that all submissions, whether written or oral, are logically structured and as succinct as possible;

- presenting the evidence in a manner which facilitates the task of the tribunal in establishing the facts that are relevant for its decision;
- assisting the tribunal in understanding the legal and technical rules relevant for the resolution of the dispute;
- ensuring that evidence and argument on legal and technical matters are not presented in a misleading manner; and
- assisting the tribunal in understanding the cultural, commercial and technical context in which the client and other protagonists conduct their business and the perspective in which they perceive the case."

As for the relation between counsel and the client, the ASA Charter sets out a number of thoughts and ends with the following words:

> In all cases, Counsel must retain the requisite independence from the client and avoid any uncritical personal espousal of the client's position. Although this is one of the most difficult tasks for Counsel, it is of paramount importance and constitutes one of the most effective hallmarks of effective advocacy in international commercial arbitration.

So let us take a few examples of what many lawyers would consider to be good advocacy and measure these examples against the principles of the ASA Charter in the form of questions:

- Do counsel always have in mind their clients' concerns about costs and time? Are their choices sometimes self-indulgent, or worse? For example: a long, detailed and dramatic cross-examination can be very self-rewarding for counsel, but does the outcome always justify the investment in everyone's time and money?
- Do counsel always have the openness of mind to understand the different cultural and legal background of their clients and of arbitrators? For example, does the principle "never ask a question if you don't know the answer" in cross examination truly foster "effective" advocacy when counsel should know that the arbitrators will have studied the file in detail before the hearing, and are thus likely to know the answer too?

- In certain jurisdictions, for some lawyers and even for certain clients, a gloves-off and aggressive approach is the hallmark of "good" advocacy. Are all counsel sufficiently flexible to adjust to the needs of international arbitration and adopt a more low-key approach? This is particularly true where the impulse for aggressive pleadings and tactics comes from the client: can counsel keep the necessary distance and independence of mind?
- Very importantly, counsel have at their disposal a broad range of procedural instruments, in particular in relation to the taking of evidence. Do counsel always have the courage to drop non-essentials and focus on the essentials? Like a virtuoso before a piano, counsel may take pride in mastery of procedural devices; but does this equate with "effective" advocacy?

Let us be honest: there is not a single practitioner of international commercial arbitration who can claim without blushing that he or she always gets it right.[9]

2.3. Intermediate Findings

There will always be a tension between different and sometimes mutually exclusive visions of what "effective advocacy" represents. This will depend not only on the cultural and legal background of the protagonists, but also on the strategic objectives of each individual case. In other words, there is no absolute "one size fits all" approach to good advocacy in international commercial arbitration.

This was very clearly shown during the preparation of the ASA Conference and at the conference itself. The first panel, composed of Bruce Gailey (providing the client's view), Professor Gabrielle Kaufmann-Kohler (providing the arbitrator's perspective) and Messrs Michael Young and Martin Burkhardt (representing counsel of Common Law and Civil Law tradition, respectively), gave varying answers to certain key questions. For example, whilst many insisted on counsel's duty to attempt forcefully to tailor the proceedings to the needs of the individual case, Martin Burkhardt struck a note of caution: "Forcefully twisting the procedure to meet the perceived needs of the party's case may raise doubts about the case's merits". All of the panelists agreed that the respective weight given to written or

---

[9] We arbitration practitioners will no doubt find solace in the wise words of Osgood Fielding III: "Well, nobody's perfect!"

oral advocacy will depend on the legal background of counsel and, perhaps more importantly, of arbitrators. Regarding the effectiveness of "open" or "closed" questions in cross examination, it was (unexpectedly, perhaps) the representative of the Common Law tradition, Michael Young, who recognised most clearly that "open" questions are hugely effective when used properly.

That said, there was significant common ground on many approaches. One area of agreement was that, with regard to witness evidence, "less is more", if only because of the risks that are inherent to putting witness on the stand: it was pointed out that counsel should never overestimate their own capacity to anticipate the testimony of their own witnesses—and never underestimate opposing counsel's lack of control over their witnesses. All panelists also agreed that aggressiveness is not appropriate, and that it should never be confused with forcefulness.

Finally, there were some surprising and unanticipated observations. Gabrielle Kaufmann-Kohler noted that a good advocate must possess intellectual courage (in the face of the opposite party, but also in the face of his or her own client or even of the arbitral tribunal). She also noted that physical stamina is an important component of good advocacy—something that anyone having experienced marathon-style hearings will readily understand and endorse. Another unexpected remark was Michael Young's inclusion of a sense of humour among the key qualities of a good advocate, because it "often engenders a sense of perspective".

3. SELECTED PITFALLS IN ADVOCACY

3.1. Context: "I Can, Therefore I Must"

Having defined what is to be understood as "advocacy" for the purpose of this article, we now turn to three examples of pitfalls that await practitioners of international commercial arbitration, two of which will be examined in detail. Before doing so, a few explanations are necessary to put our analysis into context.

The most commonly voiced complaint about international commercial arbitration is that it is too expensive and lengthy. One frequently hears that counsel are chiefly to blame for this state of affairs.[10] Reverting to the provocative mode used in the introduction to

---

[10] This article does not venture any apportionment of blame in this respect. Suffice it to note that unreasonably high costs or long procedures can be the product not only of timesheet-minded lawyers, but also of excessively belligerent parties (who are insufficiently restrained by their counsel), of arbitrators who shy from taking difficult

this article, the author draws a comparison between advocacy in international commercial arbitration and the practice of medicine. Indeed, it is a platitude to note that medical costs are soaring; it is usually doctors who are blamed. The multiplication of tests, the use of highly sophisticated but expensive equipment, second opinions and the like, taken in conjunction with the threat of malpractice litigation, have resulted in a perceived attitude that could be summarised as "I can, therefore I must."

Regrettably, a similar phenomenon has surfaced in international commercial arbitration. Counsel have in their arsenal a multitude of devices, especially in the fact-finding phase of the proceedings that, when used discerningly, can be very effective. "Effective", in this context, means for instance that they assist the arbitral tribunal in getting to the bottom of the facts, or that they contribute in making complicated issues easier to understand for the arbitrators. Three examples come to mind immediately: document production, expert evidence and site visits.

When misused, these devices rank among the worst offenders in the rogues' gallery of time- and money-wasting procedural shenanigans. "Misuse" can of course be deliberate: as already noted above, a party's strategic objective in arbitration proceedings can be to cause delay and to force the opposite party to spend considerable money on the case. However, "misuse" can also be unintentional and result from the "I can, therefore I must" mind-set.

Regarding document production, volumes have been written on this subject and the author will merely make a few general comments. Suffice it to state here that, whilst document production can be a very effective advocacy tool, all too often requests for document production are typical of the "I can, therefore I must" approach. This is especially

---

decisions early in the process or who do not enforce their own rules, and of arbitral institutions whose administrative charges can sometimes represent 50% of the fees paid to an arbitrator. Moreover, the mere fact that the fees of counsel almost always represent by far the largest single cost item in commercial arbitration is hardly surprising: among all of the participants in the proceedings, counsel will, by the very nature of their role, spend by far the most time on the case. There is nothing wrong with this as such. Significant time well devoted to a case by counsel can even reduce the work for others. For example, the ASA Charter exhorts counsel to sort the wheat from the chaff, and thus to prune their case down to what is truly worthy of the arbitrators' attention. If done well, this "boiling down" exercise results in the arbitrators never seeing the significant volumes of documents and never hearing the long explanations that were provided to counsel (and sometimes even to party-appointed experts) during the sorting-out phase. To do all of this takes significant time and effort. That said, the lesson to be taken from the proportion of legal fees compared to other costs is probably that this is an area in which there significant room for improvement.

true where document production constitutes a discrete phase of the proceedings (i.e., there are specific deadlines for requests, answers to such requests, Redfern Schedules and the like, coming after or, worse, before exchanges of briefs). In this case, counsel tend to ask the question "What could I possibly ask for?" instead of "What do I really need to ask for?".[11]

Expert evidence and site visits deserve more detailed examination.

3.2. Expert Evidence

Articles 5 and 6 of the 2010 IBA Rules on the Taking of Evidence in International Arbitration (the "IBA Rules") relate, respectively, to party-appointed experts and to tribunal-appointed experts. The detailed provisions on this subject cover no less than three pages of the total eleven pages occupied by the IBA Rules (excluding the preamble and the definitions). This gives the reader an idea of the potential importance and intricacy of the subject. To use a perfect *non sequitur*, it also illustrates the point that is made here: the resort to expert evidence is a good example of the "I can, therefore I must" mind-set.

The panelists cited above all agreed, with regard to expert evidence, that "less is more" and that counsel sometimes file expert evidence either where there is no need, or beyond what is needed. One good example (taken from the author's experience) is the filing expert evidence on the law in which the arbitrators are trained. To take an example taken from an actual case, does an arbitral tribunal formed of experienced Swiss lawyers truly need to receive expert evidence on relatively simple issues of Swiss contract law?[12] Even if one leaves the field of legal issues and enters that of technical or financial matters,

---

[11] One way of avoiding or at least mitigating this risk is to build document production into the pre-hearing written submissions. In each party's first brief on the merits, each request for document production must be announced and put into context in the factual narrative (so that the requesting party can spot the true "gaps" in its documentary evidence and so that the arbitral tribunal can easily understand the context and relevance of the requested documents), with the other conditions for document production (i.e., documents in possession of the requested party and not in possession of the requesting party, proportionality, etc.) being addressed in a separate chapter at the end of the brief. Experience shows that this way of proceeding (strongly advocated by the author when he acts as arbitrator) considerably limits the scope of document production and enables the parties to focus on what they "*must*" request, instead of on what they "*can*" request.

[12] The question was whether a contractual provision explicitly providing for one party's right to terminate in case of delayed payments required, implicitly, that the terminating party actually establish prejudice resulting from late payment in order to be entitled to exercise its termination rights, irrespective of any "abuse of right" (the answer was obviously "no").

does the fact that the case is complicated for counsel to understand without the assistance of an expert mean that the arbitral tribunal will also need the expert's pedagogy to make its findings?

Whilst it is undisputable that expert evidence may be helpful in this regard, counsel must never lose sight of the fact that it is counsel's primary responsibility to explain the case to the arbitrators. This was aptly put by Michael Young, who included among the main features of good advocacy "an ability to make complex matters simple". Counsel cannot simply subcontract this role to experts: Bruce Gailey noted that "some lawyers nearly abdicate the case to the experts" and that "this was going too far". Where counsel make excessive use of expert evidence, merely because they believe that the issues are too complicated for a lawyer to present, this obviously has adverse consequences for the process in terms of increased costs and time.[13] However, it can have more insidious repercussions: counsel unwittingly fail to make the effort to understand the issues for which they have retained experts. This, in turn, prevents counsel from presenting the case effectively.[14]

Worse, one all too frequently sees expert evidence filed in support of allegations of fact that are irrelevant under the contract or under the governing law. Two examples illustrate this:

- Sub-Clause 20.1 of the FIDIC Conditions of Contract (whatever the colour) provides that the Contractor must issue a notice of intent to claim within 28 days from becoming aware of circumstances that would entitle it to additional payment or extension of time for completion. In international practice, this time limit is a genuine "guillotine": after expiry of the 28 days, the Contractor forfeits any right to additional payment or extension of time for completion. Under most legal systems, this cut-off mechanism is legally enforceable. Unfortunately, counsel sometimes lose sight of these contractual and legal principles and file extensive expert evidence on, for instance, extensions of time for completion

---

13 These costs and additional time being: the experts' fees; the time taken by counsel in preparing the evidence with the expert; the time taken by the arbitral tribunal to digest the expert evidence; the time taken by all participants to examine the experts at the hearing; the time devoted by counsel to the processing of the experts' evidence in the post-hearing phase; the time taken by the arbitral tribunal to review the experts' evidence when weighing the evidence, deliberating the case and drafting the award.

14 Which is the opposite of the famous aphorism by the French poet and critic Nicolas Boileau: "Ce que l'on conçoit bien s'énonce clairement, et les mots pour le dire arrivent aisément" (What is well conceived is clearly expressed and the words to say it come easily).

although the Contractor clearly failed to give notice within the 28 days.

- Under Swiss law, the non-defaulting party to a contract has several remedies at its disposal if the other party is in default. One of these remedies is to rescind the contract retroactively and to claim damages corresponding to what is called, in Swiss legal jargon, the "negative interest in the entering into of the contract". This somewhat esoteric terminology relates to damages in which the rescinding party seeks to be put into the financial situation it would have been in had it never entered into the contract. The items typically claimed when exercising this remedy are the costs of negotiating the contract and expenses incurred (for naught) in view of performance under the contract. This remedy is axiomatically the opposite of claiming for the benefit of the contract, in particular loss of profit. However, this axiomatic opposition does not prevent some counsel from claiming for lost profits even when the contract has been rescinded retroactively—and filing complicated expert evidence to establish the loss of profit.[15]

Finally, perhaps one of the most dangerous pitfalls awaiting counsel is the tit-for-tat reflex, which is often on display in connection with expert evidence. It is sometimes difficult for counsel to resist the temptation to file expert evidence merely because the opponent has done so. This can be due to a number of factors, ranging from an imperfect grasp of the issues of the case to strong pressure from the client.[16] Whatever the cause, the reflex is unhealthy—and was clearly identified as such by the panelists, in particular Michael Young.

3.3. Site Visits

Site visits, just as any other form of visual inspection,[17] can be a highly efficient procedural tool. This is particularly true in construction or engineering matters. Arbitrators and counsel will almost always

---

[15] Conversely, where a party upholds the contract and seeks damages corresponding to the benefit of the deal, one sometimes also see claims for reimbursement of the expenses that the claimant party incurred in view of performing the contract – and expert evidence to support the computation of the claim for these expenses.

[16] And, perhaps, a certain degree of spinelessness on the part of counsel in the face of the client.

[17] The author was once very helpfully enlightened on the various hues of the colour white when presented with samples of powders used in the cosmetics industry.

have a better understanding of the case when they have actually seen the subject matter of the dispute (for example visit of a production line in order better to understand the logical sequence of equipment; visit of a construction site to understand the constraints in terms of available space, layout or geotechnical features; visit of completed works to visualise the nature or the extent of defects or damage to neighbouring premises; etc.).

Even in other fields, site visits can be useful. For example, where a party to an agreement has a duty of maintenance or is otherwise obligated to upkeep the value of premises (for example a hotel management agreement in which the operator must carry out renovation works regularly to ensure a continuous level of quality measured against objective standards), visual on-site inspection can be one way of determining whether this duty has been fulfilled, or conversely of understanding better why this was not possible (or did not achieve the desired result). Similarly, on-site inspection can serve, for example, to verify whether a party has complied with contractual standards for safekeeping of data.

In addition, if a site visit takes place at an early stage of the proceedings, a succinct and user-friendly report of the site visit prepared by the arbitral tribunal, with clearly referenced photographs (preferably taken by the arbitral tribunal), technical explanations and even floor-plans, can be of great value later. It can serve as a common reference for the parties' written submissions in order to situate certain issues in their physical context. The report and photographs taken on that occasion can also be a very useful aid at hearings; it is not uncommon to have the most topical photographs on the wall of the hearing room for ease of reference throughout testimonial and expert evidence.[18]

Unfortunately, the "I can, therefore I must" mind-set has a creeping tendency to manifest itself in relation to site visits as well. Given the usually significant costs attached to site visits (not only the travel and accommodation costs, but also the time spent by counsel and arbitrators in preparing, attending and following up on the visit), this can lead to very unfortunate results.

The source of the problem is very often a lack of clarity as to the purpose of the site visit. There are basically two options: either the site visit (a) serves generally to educate the arbitral tribunal, counsel and,

---

[18] Given these manifold benefits of site visits, it is perhaps surprising that the IBA Rules devote only one single paragraph of nine lines to this subject. This stands in stark contrast to the lengthy provisions on witnesses of fact, party-appointed experts and tribunal-appointed experts.

frequently, tribunal-or party appointed experts, or (b) is part of the actual taking of evidence to prove or disprove the parties' factual allegations. The distinction is crucial and has very important consequences:

- The distinction has *legal* consequences. If the site visit serves as a full-fledged means of taking evidence, the arbitral tribunal may later rely on what it saw (or heard, or smelled) during the visit to make findings of fact and thereby decide on the dispute. This, in turn means that the fundamental principles of procedural fairness and equal treatment in the taking of evidence, including the parties' right to participate actively in the taking of evidence, apply to site visits. Failure by the arbitral tribunal to guarantee these minimum standards of procedural fairness can result in the setting aside of the award.[19] This also means that where the site visit serves as a means of taking evidence, the arbitral tribunal must have zero-tolerance policy towards manipulation or stonewalling. It happens all too frequently that the party having control of the premises to be visited carefully orchestrates the site visit, which then degenerates into a crude propaganda ploy. The only way to prevent this is to order that both parties (with or without their counsel depending on the facts of each case) prepare the site visit jointly. If this is not possible due to a party's obstruction or if, for any other reason, the arbitral tribunal has the impression that what it viewed at the site visit was somewhat staged, it must discard the visit as evidence; arbitrators can also sanction the delinquent party when ruling on costs.[20]

- The distinction also has *practical* consequences. If the purpose of the site visit is merely to educate, it should take place early in the proceedings, so that the advantages described above (better understanding of the issues; availability of a well-prepared and well-documented report for future reference) benefit the parties and the arbitral tribunal from the outset. By contrast, if the site visit is an evidence-taking measure, it should not take place before the arbitral tribunal knows which facts are disputed and (at least potentially) relevant

---

19 This is the case, for example in Switzerland, under the longstanding practice of the Swiss Federal Supreme Court. See for example the decision of the Federal Supreme Court 4A_6000/2010 of 7 March 2011, para. 4.1 and references.

20 *See* for example Articles 9.2(g) and 9.7 of the IBA Rules.

> and not proven otherwise. The site visit must then focus on those facts; it makes no sense to take evidence on issues that are not even potentially irrelevant, or that are not disputed or that are proven by other means. At the beginning of the proceedings, the arbitral tribunal generally cannot know which facts are (at least potentially) relevant and disputed, let alone which allegations are already proven by other means.[21]

Regrettably, when counsel propose site visits, they do not always have in mind these fundamental distinctions and issues. Counsel will know the potential benefits of the site visit; hence the *"I can"*. However, counsel do not always think through sufficiently what the purpose of the site visit should be. In such cases, the question *"Must I*? often receives a *"yes"* answer by default. When this happens, and if the confusion as to the purpose of the site visit is not understood and dispelled by the arbitral tribunal, this can lead to serious problems.

At best, the site visit will in such cases be a waste of time and money. However, failure properly to address the issues described above can have for more serious consequences. It can lead to misunderstandings and thereby create scope for dispute at a later stage in the proceedings. This in turn generates additional and unnecessary costs. In the worst-case scenario, it can result in the situation in which the final award cites the site visit to support findings of fact that are adverse to a party that had understood the purpose of the site visit to be purely "educational" (and that party would have approached the whole matter very differently, for example in terms of staffing, preparation and recording, had it known that the arbitral tribunal would rely on the visit to make findings of fact in its award).

Even where there is clarity on the purpose of a site visit, the "I can, therefore I must" attitude can lead to waste of time and money, simply because visual inspections are not as indispensable as they are sometimes made out to be. For example, it is not always difficult for experienced arbitrators to understand differences in construction concepts on the basis of drawings or other documentary evidence, including photographs. Where arbitrators are capable of making this assessment on the basis of the written record, there is no need to conduct a site visit to establish that the works as set out in an initial design are different from what was ultimately built. Unfortunately,

---

21 These considerations mean that it could even be advisable to conduct two sites visits: an "educational" visit early in the proceedings and an "evidentiary" inspection once the tribunal has a clear idea of what is relevant and disputed. Obviously, given the cost of two visits, this would be an option only where the arbitral tribunal's assessment of the cost-benefit ratio justifies the expense.

given the good reputation that site visits enjoy, this assessment is not always carried out critically.

Finally, the "I can, therefore I must" mind-set is also on display where parties do not sufficiently consider the implications of a site visit for their own case. Take a (fictional) example: a site visit requested by the contractor to prove that construction was impossible on the owner's land, although in the meantime the owner had the construction completed by another contractor. This type of own-goal would hardly qualify as "effective" advocacy.

To conclude on site visits, the bottom line is that counsel must always form a very clear idea of what they are seeking and why. They must also make sure that this understanding is shared by all other participants in the process, not least by the arbitral tribunal. On this basis, the site visit must be subjected to a critical cost-benefit analysis.

4. CONCLUSION

In *Board of Inland Revenue v. Haddock*, the Court of Appeals found that the House of Lords was useless and should be abolished, but that since it existed the matter might as well be sent to it for a final decision. Someone having a jaundiced view of advocacy in international commercial arbitration would apply the same approach: counsel are useless and should be banned from the process, but since they are there, we might as well let them drone on.

Happily, the ASA Conference of 29 January 2010 showed that this view would be not only uncharitable, but downright wrong. Counsel play an essential role in international arbitration. Without good advocacy, there would be no efficient resolution of disputes. However, the unanimous acceptance of this (hardly original) finding does not mean that there exists a universal recipe for advocacy, let alone for "good" advocacy. First, the very term "advocacy" can be understood to have many different meanings. Second, and by far more importantly, "good" or "effective" advocacy shares at least one feature with beauty: it is in the eyes of the beholder. Third and finally, one cannot over-emphasise the warnings set out above against the "I can, therefore I must" mind-set, which is a permanent and very serious trap not only for counsel, but also for the whole process.

The author will conclude with an exhortation and simple proposition to counsel in international commercial arbitration. It is submitted here that the key to effective advocacy is for counsel always to ask themselves: "Why am I doing this—what is my goal?" "Does this goal fit into the overall case strategy, and if so how?" "What is the cost of seeking to achieve my goal?" "Have I achieved my goal?"

"Have I achieved enough to stop?" These may sound like simplistic tests, and the author would not dare claim that they are even remotely original. What they amount to is to transpose into international commercial arbitration a well-known phrase taken from François Rabelais's *Pantagruel*: "Science sans conscience n'est que ruine de l'âme" —which requires no translation.

ASA Advocacy Prize (2010) Awarded to Franz Schwarz

Laudatio

Bernard Hanotiau

Dear Colleagues,

It is for me a great honor to present the *laudatio* for this first ASA Prize for Advocacy in International Commercial Arbitration.

Before addressing the merits of the laureate, I will take the liberty of doing first the *laudatio* of ASA itself.

Last week, I was interviewed for the television in Singapore at the occasion of the opening of Maxwell Chambers and the journalist asked me what could effectively be done by Singapore to become a major venue of international arbitration. I answered that in my opinion, in order to be a very successful venue for international arbitration, you need to have very good hardware and very good software. The hardware is composed of many items such as an "easy-to-reach place", convenient facilities, flexible, arbitration-oriented legislation and a judiciary which does not interfere with arbitration except when it is so requested or where it is indispensable for the protection of fundamental values or principles. But the hardware is not enough. You also need very good software: a substantial number of law firms and lawyers motivated by, and dedicated to, international arbitration; prominent scholars who contribute by their writings and their teaching to the development of international arbitration and to the emergence of new talents; and finally, last but not least, a strong, well-administered and ambitious arbitration association which plays the role of meeting point for all generations of arbitrators, a place where know-how is exchanged and hot topics are debated. And my final comment to the journalist—which I reiterated a few hours later to the Minister of Justice who had invited a few arbitrators to discuss the same issue—was that the best example I could give of a country having the best possible hardware and software was Switzerland. And I would add that one of the main engines behind Switzerland's success story is the dynamic and innovative Swiss Arbitration Association which, year after year, under the guidance of very dynamic presidents, has been able to profile itself as the most active, creative, imaginative, arbitration association, a breeding ground for new ideas and new talents.

And it is again in this spirit that ASA has decided to create the ASA Prize for Advocacy in International Commercial Arbitration whose objective is to encourage Counsel who, through their exceptional talents in advocacy, contribute most effectively to the Association's objective of promoting the effective resolution of international commercial disputes through arbitration. Congratulations to ASA for this initiative.

What are the qualities of a good Counsel in an arbitration case? They have been superbly enunciated in the ASA Charter of Advocacy in International Commercial Arbitration. Everyone should read them carefully because they are a very good summary of what an arbitral tribunal expects from Counsel in an arbitration procedure.

But let us now come to our laureate.

I am extremely pleased that ASA has decided to grant its first Prize to Franz Schwarz, considering that he is a clear illustration of all the qualities expected from a talented arbitration lawyer in the new generation.

Franz Schwarz is indeed quite a young lawyer, still in his thirties but all lawyers and arbitrators who had the privilege of seeing him in action in arbitration procedures agree that he is definitely one of the best lawyers of his generation, somebody that you will hear more and more about in arbitration circles in the years to come.

Franz received his first law degree, graduating top of his class, at the University of Vienna, School of Law, in 1995, and subsequently completed his post graduate studies at the London School of Economics in 1999. He has qualified as Rechtsanwalt in Austria and is presently a partner in the litigation department of a major American law firm and a Vice Chair of its International Arbitration Practice Group. Franz is presently based in London but acts as Counsel both in civil law and common law procedures, and in ad hoc arbitrations as well as arbitrations conducted according to the rules of the ICC, the LCIA, the Vienna and Stockholm Chambers of Commerce to take just a few examples. Beyond his role in arbitration procedures, Franz also counsels clients on conflict of laws issues and international enforcement of arbitration awards and judgements, in commercial as well as in investment cases.

According to the ASA Charter of Advocacy, as was emphasised this morning, effective advocacy in international commercial arbitration is above all about communication with the tribunal, understanding its task and assisting the tribunal in meeting its obligation. This implies among other things making a clear, concise and user friendly presentation of the case, ensuring that all submissions, whether written or oral, are logically structured and as succinct as possible, presenting the evidence in a manner which facilitates the task of the panel in establishing the facts that are relevant for the decision and assisting the tribunal in understanding the legal and technical rules relevant for the resolution of the dispute, as well as the cultural, commercial and technical context in which the parties conduct their business.

This is what arbitrators who had the pleasure of having Franz appearing in front of them as Counsel, have experienced. They confirm that he is of great assistance to the panel, that he presents his clients' position in a very clear and efficient way, that when the tribunal tells him that it is sufficiently informed of a certain aspect of the case, he immediately stops his cross-examination and turns to another topic. Lawyers and arbitrators who have seen him in action confirm that they have been extremely impressed by his exceptional talent. He can plead a case alone from A to Z during a full week, cross-examining all the witnesses efficiently and with great skill.

One of the other qualities enunciated by the ASA Charter is for Counsel to have a true international approach to international arbitration and arbitral procedure, not sticking to the local procedure in which Counsel has been educated—as is unfortunately still often the case in some jurisdictions—but approaching the case from a genuinely international perspective.

Again, those who have seen Franz acting as Counsel confirm that it is undoubtedly another quality that he brilliantly demonstrates, probably due to his dual training and education in the Austrian and English law systems. And Franz confirms this approach himself in the major treatise on International Arbitration in Austria that he published last year with Christian Konrad: "... this book recognizes that in today's world, a discussion of national arbitration law is incomplete without recourse to international practice and procedures. Transnational disputes must be mindful of, and respect, the often different cultural and legal backgrounds and expectations of the parties, their counsel and the arbitrators. This book ... draws from, and seeks to reconcile, processes available in civil and common law jurisdictions in order to serve the overriding goal of ensuring that arbitration remains predictable, expeditious and fair".

This is clearly a "profession de foi" that Franz applies when he acts as Counsel in international arbitration procedures.

In the quotation that I just read, Franz Schwarz says that one of the ultimate goals of arbitration is to be fair; and indeed, we will all agree, fairness has to be omnipresent in arbitration: as reminded by the ASA Charter of Advocacy, not only must the process be fair but Counsel must also demonstrate fairness in his relationship to the other players in the arbitration procedure. Counsel should refrain from ambush tactics, should refrain from aggressiveness, should treat the other party's advocates, witnesses and experts with dignity and courtesy. Counsel should also avoid personal attacks: they are not only counterproductive, they are against the spirit of international arbitration. Lawyers and arbitrators who have experienced Franz in international arbitration confirm that he behaves himself as a gentleman, with great intellectual honesty, in the most courteous way and when he expresses, rarely, what the French would refer to as "une petite pique", it is always done within acceptable limits and in a very elegant way.

Again, those who have seen Franz Schwarz act as Counsel in an international arbitration report that they have been impressed by his efficiency, his clarity, his mastery of the procedure, his commitment to the defense of the case, his determination but also his flexibility. They confirm that he is definitely one of the most talented lawyers of the new generation of arbitration—and indeed, he has been so identified in the most recent expert guides. Chambers UK reports that he has "a razor-sharp written style", Chambers Europe refers to him as "a star in the making" and as "a convincing and dynamic individual, with a remarkably sharp mind".

And, as if lawyering was not enough, Franz has, in the continuation of his work as Counsel, published last year with a colleague a one thousand page treatise on International Arbitration in Austria. Those who read the book have been impressed by the know-how and maturity that he is demonstrating. This is a further confirmation, if needed, that ASA made the right decision in granting him their first Prize for Advocacy in International Commercial Arbitration.

You may have asked yourself the question: does Franz Schwarz know that he is a very talented lawyer? The reports that ASA has received tend to lead to an affirmative answer. First, when you are that good, it is difficult to conceive that you do not realize that you are a brilliant lawyer. But there is one element which cannot mislead: the lawyers and arbitrators who have been consulted confirm that, at various points during his oral arguments or cross-examination of witnesses, Franz has the habit of saying that he apologizes for the quality of his English. You will have noticed, as I have, that his English is just perfect. There is therefore only one interpretation of this little element of *pédanterie* and it is the following. In reality, Franz is telling us: "gentlemen, you have realized how good my English is. But don't forget that it is not my mother tongue which is German".

Yes, we are convinced that Franz Schwarz is conscious that he is a very talented Counsel.

Franz, we wish you the greatest possible success and we hope and expect that beyond your work as Counsel, you will be in the years to come and during all your career, an advocate of the objectives and values that the Swiss Arbitration Association sought to promote among young lawyers by creating the ASA Advocacy Prize. And once again, congratulations for a well-deserved award.

ASA Advocacy Prize (2012) Awarded to Philippe Pinsolle

Laudatio

Henry Peter

Dear Colleagues, dear Friends, dear Philippe,

Probably much more than in ordinary proceedings, Counsel have a key role to play in the arbitral process. This requires many and exceptional skills. It is these skills that form effective advocacy; these skills that give their "lettres de noblesse" to arbitration and probably justify its existence; these skills that, through the "ASA Prize for Advocacy in International Commercial Arbitration", ASA seeks to honour and promote.

Being clear, concise, realistic, friendly and user-friendly; going to the point both in fact and law; facilitating the tasks of the tribunal; being fair and not misleading; being sober, respectful, not confrontational; acting with style, courtesy and dignity; avoiding personal attacks; being critically objective, always independent: these are some of the many qualities required, some of which, unfortunately, are "en voie de disparition".

I am told that, this year, ASA's selection committee had many very strong candidates. The choice may not have been easy. What is certain is that they recognised that "rare breed", the "oiseau rare", the ideal candidate, and that they have made a totally convincing choice.

Philippe Pinsolle is known to most of us. He studied in Paris and Oxford; he is admitted both in Paris and in England, as a Barrister. He joined Shearman & Sterling some 20 years ago where he is now a partner playing a central role in the firm's international arbitration group in Paris.

Although still quite young, Philippe already has an impressive track record. He has acted as counsel in more than 150 international arbitration cases, some of which of significant importance. He has been chairman, sole arbitrator and party appointed arbitrator in numerous proceedings.

Several years ago, as a Counsel, I had the chance to work against him. Shortly thereafter an important and demanding client of mine needed assistance in a difficult case in Paris: guess who I selected? Philippe of course! This sequence of event is probably more telling than many words.

Philippe is the author of numerous articles in the field of international arbitration, both in French and in English. He is often called to deliver speeches or teach and he is member of an impressive number of respected associations, when not member or chairman of their boards.

He certainly had the privilege of working closely, for years, with an exceptional Maestro, Prof. Emmanuel Gaillard. Some "*mauvaises langues*" suggested that Philippe would never be able to get out of Emmanuel's cumbersome shadow. They were proven wrong.

Philippe is a true talent of his own. He combines a British style with a touch of French aristocracy. Because of his south west of France origin, his DNA contains a mixture of *foie gras* and rugby: this explains why he is at the same time a refined gentlemen and a tough fighter. More generally, Philippe is a successful combination of cultures, qualities and styles, which makes him truly outstanding in his generation.

But, all this, still does not completely convey that little something that Philippe has and that makes him so efficient and respected. That little something that enables him to be appreciated at the same time by his clients, by arbitral tribunals and even by his opponents. Perhaps will he once tell us what it is that makes him different—his secret weapon?

In any event, Philippe is the synthesis of these qualities and skills that make an ideal Counsel in commercial arbitration. He is the prototype of what the ASA Prize has been conceived for.

Philippe, you are contributing a lot to our noble venture. Today's seminar is about quick, efficient and fair dispute resolution. By your behaviour, you are the personification of these values. I am pleased and honoured to have been invited to deliver this *laudatio* for a well-deserved award.

PART II

The Advocates: Roles and Rules for Counsel

Professional Conduct in International Arbitration – A Discipline of Its Own for a Discipline of Its Kind

Matthew Gearing and Sheila Ahuja

1. INTRODUCTION

When Prof. Catherine A. Rogers wrote on this topic in 2002, she noted that international arbitration "dwells in an ethical no-man's land."[1]

A common feature in the practice of every lawyer around the world is professional conduct regulation. Lawyers across all jurisdictions are subject to certain rules which regulate their conduct in the practice of their profession. Most, if not all, jurisdictions have their own set of rules governing the conduct of those lawyers who are admitted into that jurisdiction. In many but not all cases these rules continue to bind a lawyer irrespective of where he or she chooses to practice. Thus although the principle of applying each of these rules is largely territorial, their application in some situations is extra-territorial.

Professional conduct regulation is also territorial in the sense that a lawyer may be subject to the rules of the jurisdiction in which he or she chooses to practice, just by virtue of being physically located in that jurisdiction and even if not qualified in that jurisdiction. Thus a practising lawyer could at any certain point in time be subject to multiple rules in multiple jurisdictions, the connection in most cases resulting from one type of territorial connection or another with such jurisdiction.

While a territorial-based approach is completely logical in the territorial-based platform of national court litigation, this approach is not easily translated into international arbitration. International arbitration by its very nature involves arbitration lawyers from different jurisdictions coming together before what is more likely than not an internationally-composed arbitral tribunal seated in a jurisdiction that very often bears no connection to any of the parties. This begs the question as to what is the best approach to regulate the professional activities of lawyers in international arbitration. While that may be an interesting question, most interesting questions are

---

1 Rogers, Fit and Function in Legal Ethics: Developing a Code of Conduct for International Arbitration.

labelled so for lack of an obvious answer. This is most certainly one of them.

The obvious answer to avoid this tangled web of complications would be to establish one set of rules by which all lawyers practising international arbitration are bound—a discipline of its own for a discipline of its kind. But developing such rules and conferring binding effect on them is a far from easy task. How does one set of rules adapt to a wide range of varying, and potentially conflicting, jurisdictions around the world? Arguably, the rules would have to be of a generic enough nature to serve a 'one size fits all' purpose. But if so would they serve any real or substantive purpose? Or would they effectively be disregarded for the comparatively detailed provisions of the jurisdiction then in question? We address this concern in further detail below. Another concern is one of potential conflict between different sets of rules which provide for the same or similar issues. What happens if there is a clash between a uniform set of rules and the existing rules to which the arbitration lawyer is subject in his/her jurisdiction? Should the international standard prevail in the event of a conflict? Even if it did, would the lawyer be reprimanded for non-compliance with the rules of his/her jurisdiction, since as discussed below, the latter would have to be complied with in addition to the international standard?

As such, in the absence of any current binding international standard, to which rules should an international arbitration lawyer be subject in the conduct of international arbitration? This is a multiple choice question, and the following potential answers come to mind and each one is examined in further detail below:

(a) As with the courts, the professional conduct rules of the home Bar (the **Home Bar rules**) would likely apply in any event. The question therefore is whether these rules are sufficient so that no additional standard need be applied?

(b) Or, notwithstanding the application of the Home Bar rules, because the conduct and procedure of an arbitration is governed by the rules of the seat, should these rules of the place of arbitration apply to issues of professional conduct?

(c) Or should there, in addition to the Home Bar rules, be a new set of rules imposing a unified standard applicable to all arbitrations, irrespective of where the parties are from, in the form of international professional conduct rules?

(d) Or, notwithstanding the application of the Home Bar rules, should the question of the most appropriate rules be best left to a tribunal to determine on a case-by-case basis?

2. THE MULTIPLE CHOICE OF RULES

2.1. Application of the Professional Conduct Rules of the Home Bar

Generally, the professional conduct rules of the jurisdiction in which a lawyer is qualified, the Home Bar rules, will govern the professional practice of that lawyer even where the lawyer is at the time practising in a foreign jurisdiction. However, whether the Home Bar rules of his/her Home Bar jurisdiction also extend to that lawyer's practice in an international arbitration seated in a foreign jurisdiction would depend on the scope of the relevant Home Bar rules.

The first key consideration here is whether these Home Bar rules expressly extend to the practice of arbitration. Some rules expressly provide that they do,[2] whilst other rules do so implicitly.[3] Assuming that the Home Bar Rules do apply to the conduct of an arbitration, the next question is whether they purport to have extra-territorial effect.

For example, the Hong Kong Solicitors' Guide to Professional Conduct (the **Hong Kong Solicitors' Guide**) states that "A Hong Kong solicitor when practising as a Hong Kong solicitor outside Hong Kong remains bound by the general principles of professional conduct which apply to him as a Hong Kong solicitor."[4]

Under the Legal Profession (Professional Conduct) Rules applicable to Singaporean advocates and solicitors, a Court is defined as including a tribunal and includes no territorial restriction. So the duties which an advocate or solicitor assumes to the Court, including for example the duty to inform it of all relevant legal provisions, whether favourable to his client's case or not, would apply as a duty to

---

[2] The EC Code of Conduct for Lawyers states at Rule 4.5: "The rules governing a lawyer's relations with the courts apply also to his relations with arbitrators...." We can also see a similar principle in the Règlement intérieur du Barreau de Paris at Article 6.2, which states: "il doit en outre veiller au respect des règles particulières qui régissent la procédure arbitrale".

[3] For example, the 2011 England and Wales Solicitors Regulation Authority Code of Conduct refers to an English solicitor's practice before a 'tribunal'.

[4] Rule 1.06, Chapter 1, The Hong Kong Solicitor's Guide to Professional Conduct, Second Edition.

the tribunal where that Singaporean advocate or solicitor appears in an arbitration anywhere in the world.[5]

Chapter 5 of the 2011 England and Wales Solicitors Regulation Authority Code of Conduct on conduct in litigation and advocacy extends to an English qualified solicitor's overseas practice in relation to litigation or advocacy conducted before a "a court, tribunal or enquiry of England and Wales or a British court martial". A 'court' is defined in the Code as "any court, tribunal or enquiry of England and Wales, or a British court martial, or any court of another jurisdiction", which appears to have extra-territorial effect. A tribunal is not defined in the Code. This appears to create the curious outcome that this Rule extends to an English arbitral tribunal but not to a foreign-seated one.

So, erring on the side of caution, it is safe to assume that in most cases a lawyer remains subject to the rules of his Home Bar even where he appears in an arbitration outside of his own jurisdiction. However, the application of this standard alone raises some concerns that are likely to be unique to the context of international arbitration. For instance, what happens in a situation where two arbitration lawyers from different jurisdictions appear as opposing counsel in an international arbitration? If each of them is only subject to their respective Home Bar rules, there would be multiple and potentially different standards at play. More importantly, does this mean that there may be a sloping playing field which potentially affects the fair conduct of the arbitration?

2.2. Rules of the Seat of Arbitration?

The potential problem of a sloping playing field suggests that the approach of applying the Home Bar rules alone is far from ideal in international arbitration. An alternative approach, which circumvents the issue of multiple rules applying at the same time, would be to seek to superimpose above and beyond the application of the Home Bar rules one set of professional conduct rules for each arbitration. The rules of the seat of the arbitration immediately come to mind.

Since the parties adopt the law of the seat as the law governing the procedure of their arbitration, extending this application to the local standards of professional conduct has some logic. So far so good, but what are these rules? Are we referring to the professional conduct rules in force in the jurisdiction of the seat, and/or to procedural rules

---

5 Singapore Legal Profession Act (Cap. 161, Section 71), Legal Profession (Professional Conduct) Rules, see sections 3(1) and 60(c).

(if any) submitted to by the parties by which the arbitration is to be administered?

2.2.1. Professional conduct rules of the seat

By this approach, the professional conduct rules of the seat of an arbitration would apply to the conduct of all lawyers in an arbitration, in addition to their place of admission or permanent practice at the time. This concept is not unheard of. In fact, some rules expressly state that a lawyer is subject to the rules of the host place where he or she happens to be practicing, even if he or she is not qualified in that jurisdiction.

The Hong Kong Solicitors' Guide, introduced above, states in the context of a Hong Kong qualified solicitor's practice outside Hong Kong: "In the absence of an express application of local rules to the solicitor as a foreign lawyer, the solicitor should nevertheless respect the rules of conduct applied to local lawyers."[6]

This approach is adopted in the European Union. Article 2.4 of the Code of Conduct for Lawyers of the European Union of the Council of Bars and Law Societies of Europe (the **EC Code of Conduct for Lawyers**) provides that, "[w]hen practising cross-border, a lawyer from another Member State may be bound to comply with the rules of the Bar or Law Society of the host Member State". Although this Code is not in itself binding, it has been adopted at national level in many European Union Member States.[7]

However, although theoretically this provides some element of certainty as to the applicable professional conduct rules in an international arbitration, this approach is controversial.

Is it really appropriate to subject lawyers from another jurisdiction to the local bar rules of the seat of the arbitration, when those local bar rules have in all probability been designed with local requirements in mind, and are very likely to have as their central object the conduct of local court proceedings and not international arbitration?

As Gary Born states: "... it typically makes little sense to apply the rules of professional conduct applicable in local litigations in the arbitral seat to counsel in an international arbitration. In fact, it is fair to say that many counsel in international arbitrations have little

6 Commentary 3, Rule 1.06, Chapter 1, The Hong Kong Solicitor's Guide to Professional Conduct, Second Edition.

7 Article 1.3.2 of this Code provides that the rules within the Code are to be "adopted as enforceable rules", though a lawyer subject to these rules will still "remain bound to observe the rules of the Bar or Law Society to which he or she belongs to the extent that they are consistent with the rules in this Code".

concept of the local rules of professional conduct applicable in domestic courts in the arbitral seat (and less conception that these might regulate their conduct)."[8]

Besides this obvious oddity, other potentially curious consequences arise from adopting this approach.

In particular, there is the problem of a potential conflict between the application of the professional conduct rules of the seat and the Home Bar rules. As a result of applying the rules of the seat in addition to Home Bar rules, in the event that an arbitration lawyer acting as counsel in an arbitration is faced with a situation where he has complied with his Home Bar rules, but notwithstanding or as a result of such compliance he/she has breached the professional conduct rules of the seat, it would be simply unfair to penalise him for breaching the latter when he/she was acting in compliance with the former.

For instance, the New York Rules of Professional Conduct prohibit simultaneous representation for and against a client[9], whereas the Hong Kong Solicitors' Guide contains no such absolute prohibition (although the Hong Kong rules can have that effect in certain situations). Can a Hong Kong solicitor represent a client it is simultaneously acting against on an unrelated matter if the seat of the arbitration is New York, even if in so doing the Hong Kong solicitor has not breached the Hong Kong rules?

Of course, there is no clear answer to this question, other than noting that the outcome may well depend on the identity of the body called to consider the question. The relevant Home Bar association is unlikely to be able to sanction a lawyer for breaching any rules other than the relevant Home Bar rules. A domestic court at the place of qualification of the lawyer is also unlikely to take a different view. An arbitral tribunal might apply a broader approach, but that of course pre-supposes that a tribunal has any power at all to consider such questions. This question is considered further at 'Powers and Sanctions' below.

In the context of the Hong Kong example, the commentary to the Hong Kong Solicitors' Guide notes:

---

[8] GARY B. BORN, INTERNATIONAL COMMERCIAL ARBITRATION p. 2319 (Kluwer Law International 2009).

[9] Commentary 6 to Rule 1.7 states: The duty to avoid the representation of differing interest prohibits, among other things, undertaking representation adverse to a current client without that client's informed consent. For example, absent consent, a lawyer may not advocate in one matter against another client that the lawyer represents in some other matter, even when the matters are wholly unrelated.

> Where the structure and sphere of activity of the local legal profession or professions differ substantially from those of Hong Kong solicitors, it may be inappropriate or impossible for a solicitor to comply in every particular with the rules of conduct applicable to the local profession or professions, or it may be doubtful which rules of conduct should be applied. In such circumstances, the solicitor should observe the standards of conduct applicable to the local lawyers to the extent this can be done without infringing the rules applicable to Hong Kong solicitors and without hindering the proper exercise of his or her profession.

This reinforces the point that as far as the Home Bar association is concerned, compliance with the Home Bar rules is paramount, and everything else must yield to that objective.

2.2.2. Procedural rules of the place of arbitration?

An alternative approach is to look to the **procedural rules** of the seat of the arbitration (that is, as opposed to its professional conduct rules which are in any event likely to be far removed from the arbitration proceedings).

Are any applicable procedural rules sufficiently detailed to regulate the professional conduct of lawyers in international arbitration? In fact, most procedural rules in arbitration do grant the tribunal general powers to ensure the fairness and integrity of the arbitration, which could implicitly capture the power to regulate the ethical and professional standards of those involved in that arbitration. The 2012 ICC Rules of Arbitration[10] for example, state that "[i]n all cases, the Arbitral Tribunal shall act fairly and impartially and ensure that each party has a reasonable opportunity to present its case."[11] Similarly, the UNCITRAL Arbitration Rules 2010 state that an arbitral tribunal "shall conduct the proceedings so as to avoid unnecessary delay and expense and to provide a fair and efficient process for resolving the parties' dispute",[12] while the SIAC Rules 2010 state that "[t]he Tribunal shall conduct the arbitration in such manner as it considers appropriate, after consulting with the parties, to ensure the fair, expeditious, economical and final determination of the dispute".[13]

---

[10] ICC Arbitration Rules in force from 1 January 2012.

[11] Article 22.4 of the 2012 ICC Rules of Arbitration.

[12] Article 17.1 of the UNCITRAL Arbitration Rules, revised in 2010.

[13] Rule 16.1 of the Arbitration Rules of the Singapore International Arbitration Centre, 4th Edition, 1 July 2010 (**SIAC Rules 2010**).

There are also more specific provisions in these procedural rules which are intended to regulate professional conduct in the arbitration. Examples of these rules, along with areas of divergence as between the various institutions, are as follows:

2.2.3. Conflict of interest

As with most professional conduct rules,[14] institutional arbitration rules also contain a duty of disclosure of conflict in the context of international arbitration. Examples can be seen in various institutional rules, including the UNCITRAL Arbitration Rules 2010, the 2012 ICC Rules of Arbitration and the LCIA Arbitration Rules.[15] However, unlike the professional conduct rules, the duty of disclosure in arbitral procedural rules appears to only be imposed on the arbitrator, and not counsel. The International Bar Association (IBA) Working Group recommended that such a duty should extend to counsel and such a duty was incorporated into the Guidelines on Conflict of Interest in International Arbitration.[16] However, as these are mere guidelines and not nearly as onerous as binding institutional rules, does it mean that arbitration lawyers acting as counsel are free from any duty of disclosure?

2.2.4. Witness interviews and preparation

Most arbitral institutional rules contain some provision on witness evidence, which are relatively generic in nature and address in broad terms the ability of counsel to interview a witness.[17] These rules do not usually go as far as to deal with the specifics of dealing with a

---

[14] *See,* Rule 3.2 of the EC Code of Conduct for Lawyers by way of example.

[15] *See,* Article 11 of the UNCITRAL Arbitration Rules 2010, Article 7.2 of the 2012 ICC Rules of Arbitration and Article 5.3 of the London Court of International Arbitration (LCIA) Arbitration Rules.

[16] It was recommended by the IBA Working Group that a party or its agent, its counsel, have a duty to disclose. General Standard 7 of the IBA Guidelines on Conflicts of Interest in International Arbitration, 'Duty of Arbitrator and Parties', provides: "A party shall inform an arbitrator, the Arbitral Tribunal, the other parties and the arbitration institution ... about any direct or indirect relationship between it ... and the arbitrator. The party shall do so on its own initiative before the beginning of the proceeding or as soon as it becomes aware of such relationship."

[17] *See,* by way of examples Article 4(3) of the 2010 IBA Rules on the Taking of Evidence in International Arbitration, Article 25.2 of the 2012 Swiss Rules of International Arbitration and Rule 20.6 of the LCIA Arbitration Rules.

witness, for instance to deal with the conflict between various national rules on witness "preparation" or "familiarisation".[18]

2.2.5. Contingency fees

Arbitral institutional rules do not generally provide for (or against) contingency or conditional fee arrangements. In terms of professional conduct rules, contingency fees are permitted in some jurisdictions,[19] whilst being impermissible in others.[20] Then there are other jurisdictions which contain a middle ground position.[21]

So where does this leave the enforceability of a contingency or conditional fee arrangement entered into between an arbitration lawyer and his/her client? Again, the safe answer, in the absence of any authority on the point, is to assume that the agreement must be enforceable under the applicable rules of both the seat of arbitration and the lawyer's Home Bar rules.

---

18 The general position on witness preparation and familiarization in the United States is that U.S. lawyers may interview witnesses and assist in the preparation of witness testimony, subject to certain limitations. While this is subject to certain limitations, the scope of such assistance can be fairly wide. As highlighted in a recent article by Peter J. Rees, the Comments and Illustrations section of Restatement of the Law, Third, The Law Governing Lawyers, s. 116 in the United States plainly states: "A lawyer may suggest [to the witness] choice of words that might be employed to make the witness's meaning clear". (Page 519, The Revised IBA Rules of Evidence, Peter J. Rees, (2010) 76 Arbitration 3, August 2010 Chartered Institute of Arbitrators.) In England and Wales, by contrast, lawyers are not permitted to coach or train a witness. This topic has been the subject of some decisions in the criminal and civil context, to which see the following English judgments: R v. Momodou [2005] EWCA Crim 177 Court of Appeal (Criminal Division) in the criminal context, where the Court held that "the witness should give his or her own evidence, so far as practicable uninfluenced by what anyone else said..."; Ultraframe (UK) Ltd v. Fielding [2005] EWHC 1638 (Ch), paragraph 25, in the civil context, which stated that mock cross examination was permissible and although the judge declined to give general guidance on limits of witness familiarization, he placed emphasis on the principle that the evidence of the witness is his "honest and independent recollection" stating that this was key to both civil and criminal cases. To take it a step further, certain civil law jurisdictions (specifically, some jurisdictions in the European Union such as France and Germany) provide for rules to the effect that lawyers cannot contact or even attempt to affect a witness's testimony.

19 Rule 1.5(c) of the ABA Model Rules of Professional Conduct states that "[a] fee may be contingent on the outcome of the matter for which the service is rendered, except in a matter in which a contingent fee is prohibited by paragraph (d) or other law."

20 *See*, The EC Code of Conduct for Lawyers, Rule 3.3.1 and Ordre des avocats de Paris, Article 3.5.3 of the Internal Rules.

21 England and Wales for example permits only conditional fee but not contingency fee arrangements, as provided for in IB(1.17) and IB(1.27) of the 2011 England and Wales Solicitors Regulation Authority Code of Conduct.

2.2.6. Privilege and Confidentiality

Similarly, there is a lack of guidance on the issue of privilege in procedural arbitral rules. Some help is provided by the 2010 IBA Rules on the Taking of Evidence in International Arbitration, which states at Article 9(2)(b) that:

> The Arbitral Tribunal shall, at the request of a Party or on its own motion, exclude from evidence or production any document, statement, oral testimony or inspection for...legal impediment or privilege under the legal or ethical rules determined by the Arbitral Tribunal to be applicable.[22]

The result of course is that there are divergent approaches as to the application of rules of privilege and confidentiality in international arbitration. This article is not the place to consider such divergent approaches, other than noting that no set of rules, whether binding or not, come close to resolving the issue as to which rules should be applied.

2.3. International Professional Conduct Rules?

Given the problems that persist with applying any set of existing rules specific to a particular jurisdiction or arbitral institution to determine the standard of professional conduct of counsel in arbitration, the question then arises as to whether we can look to a globally uniform standard by way of a set of international rules of professional conduct.

The present contenders are the EC Code of Conduct for Lawyers or the IBA Principles for the Legal Profession adopted by the International Bar Association. Both are non-binding sets of guidelines that were put in place for the very purpose of forming a uniform standard that can be applied across all jurisdictions or in the case of the EC Code of Conduct for Lawyers, across all EC jurisdictions. Although, as we say above, the EC Code of Conduct for Lawyers is encouraged to be and has been adopted in many Member States, the Code in itself is not binding.

---

22 *See also,* the International Arbitration Rules of the International Centre for Dispute Resolution (**ICDR Rules**), Art 20(6): the tribunal shall "take into account applicable principles of legal privilege, such as those involving the confidentiality of communications between a lawyer and client". There is also provision in the ICDR Rules by which a tribunal is to have regard to applicable principles of privilege in determining the 'admissibility, relevance, materiality and weight' of evidence in the arbitration.

Whilst both of these documents are useful starting points, they do not provide anything beyond statements of generally applicable principles. They do not provide guidance as to how to resolve specific situations which might arise.

The IBA Principles for the Legal Profession are three pages in length, with 10 broadly drafted generic principles. The scope of the principles is too general in nature and these principles by no means provide the level of detail required in terms of guidance to properly serve as a prevailing set of professional conduct rules. Further, the preamble to these principles expressly states as follows:

> These General Principles are not intended to replace or limit a lawyer's obligation under applicable laws or rules of professional conduct. Nor are they to be used as criteria for imposing liability, sanctions, or disciplinary measures of any kind.

The prevailing view in arbitration circles is that arbitration could benefit from the introduction of a more detailed internationally accepted set of standards.

As Johnny Veeder said in his 2001 Goff Lecture:[23]

> The absence of enforceable standards across national boundaries threatened a possible gradual deterioration in the standards of legal professional conduct. The international arbitral process would then be brought into disrepute and, once its good reputation was lost, it could take decades to rebuild confidence.

Aware of this need, the Arbitration Committee of the International Bar Association formed a Task Force on Counsel Ethics in International Arbitration in 2008 with the purpose of "investigating the different and often contrasting ethical and cultural norms, standards and disciplinary rules that may apply to counsel in international arbitrations". The mandate of this Task Force appears to focus on the issue of whether the lack of international guidelines and conflicting norms in counsel ethics undermines the fundamental protections of fairness and equality of treatment and the integrity of international arbitration proceedings, and if it does so undermine, then what, if anything, the Task Force should propose to mitigate any such adverse impact. The Task Force held various meetings between 2009 and 2010 to develop initial views on the "threshold question" as to "whether ethical issues arise in such a manner or with sufficient frequency that

---

[23] Johnny Veeder, *Goff Lecture*, 2001.

they required to be considered further". Having concluded that further consideration was required, they have since engaged in the process of compiling research by way of a questionnaire to develop comprehensive knowledge in the area.

Of course, achieving consensus on an internationally acceptable set of professional conduct rules is easier said than done. The more detailed that such a code would seek to be, the greater the level of disagreement which would likely arise as to its content. The code could either be high level, and then risk being essentially meaningless, or more detailed, but at this level obtaining true cross border consensus would be difficult.

3. THE CONFLICT AND THE CHOICE

In the present rather confused situation, how is a tribunal meant to decide the best way forward, bearing in mind its duty to ensure procedural fairness?

The authors are aware of one unpublished ICSID[24] decision regarding a challenge to the participation of counsel in an arbitration where it was said by the tribunal that although the rules of two potential Home Bars were presented in argument for and against exclusion of a particular counsel, neither of these rules bound an international tribunal and its decision should not be based upon any of the professional ethics rules of a particular jurisdiction, but instead upon general principles of fair conduct.

It is submitted that this, for now at least, must be the right approach. Until such time as the desired rules serving as "one right answer" do come into existence and subsequent force, a tribunal retains the duty to guarantee every person procedural fairness in arbitration. It is not however an international policeman for myriad sets of bar rules. Indeed, an arbitral tribunal is granted no power to enforce any national set of bar rules and in particular would not have the power to impose coercive sanctions on counsel.

So where faced with a situation which threatens the fair or expeditious conduct of the arbitration, it is submitted that the tribunal may take action justified by reference to its duty to ensure fairness in the proceedings and to maintain the integrity of the proceedings. However, a tribunal would not usually take action lightly, and in particular may wish to act only in situations where there is no other solution to the issue.

---

[24] International Centre for Settlement of Investment Disputes.

4. THE POWERS AND SANCTIONS

So, if a tribunal might feel compelled to act in extreme situations, what powers does it have to do so, and what orders and sanctions might it pass?

4.1. Powers Derived from Procedural Rules

Most major sets of procedural rules provide for the challenge or removal of an arbitrator. See for example Articles 11 to 13 of the UNCITRAL Rules 2010, Articles 11 and 14 of the 2012 ICC Rules of Arbitration and Article 10 of the LCIA Arbitration Rules. But in the case of counsel, express power is rarely (if ever) conferred on tribunals. The same can be said of national procedural laws of arbitration in that no such power to remove or challenge advocates in arbitration exists.[25]

In the absence of an express power, can one be inferred? At least if exclusion of counsel from a hearing or from representing a party altogether is sought, as it sometimes is, the common provisions which allow freedom of choice of legal representatives need to be tackled and overcome.

For example, the UNCITRAL Rules 2010 state at Article 5:

> Each party may be represented or assisted by persons chosen by it. The names and addresses of such persons must be communicated to all parties and to the arbitral tribunal. Such communication must specify whether the appointment is being made for purposes of representation or assistance. Where a person is to act as a representative of a party, the arbitral tribunal, on its own initiative or at the request of any party, may at any time require proof of authority granted to the representative in such a form as the arbitral tribunal may determine.[26]

Consistent with the approach taken by UNCITRAL, most rules provide for a high degree of freedom to choose representatives, to the

---

[25] *See, for example,* section 24 of the English Arbitration Act 1996 which gives the English courts the power to remove an arbitrator, but contains no analogous provision for removal of counsel. Similarly, *see,* Article 180, chapter 12 of the Swiss Private International Law Act 1989 (Loi fédérale sur le droit international privé) which provides only for the challenge of arbitrators.

[26] Other examples are as follows: ICC Rules, Article 21.4: "The parties may appear in person or through duly authorized representatives. In addition, they may be assisted by advisors"; and SIAC Rules 2010, Rules 20.1: "Any party may be represented by legal practitioners or any other representatives, subject to such proof of authority as the Registrar or the Tribunal may require."

extent that even a legal qualification is not strictly necessary. Unlike in most court proceedings, a party can be represented by a director, employee, consultant or other non-legally qualified person. How far can we take this freedom though? Does freedom of choice entail a freedom to choose anyone? Does this extend to the choice of counsel who for example has advised the other party on the same or similar issues? Or a counsel who has been dis-barred? If there is such a wide discretion on the parties, how is there ever any room to imply a power on the tribunal to exclude or curtail the involvement of counsel?

Also of relevance, an arbitral tribunal has the duty to conduct proceedings fairly and expeditiously, as can be seen in the following examples:

- The arbitral tribunal ... shall conduct the proceedings so as to avoid unnecessary delay and expense and to provide a fair and efficient process for resolving the parties' dispute. (Article 17(1) UNCITRAL Rules 2010).
- An Arbitral Tribunal has a general duty "to adopt procedures suitable to the circumstances of the arbitration, avoiding unnecessary delay or expense, so as to provide a fair and efficient means for the final resolution of the parties' dispute." (Article 14.1(ii) LCIA Arbitration Rules).

Inherent in the above duty is the responsibility of the tribunal to try to ensure that no party in the arbitration behaves in a way as to offend the fairness and efficiency of the arbitral process. If a tribunal was to act to limit or curtail the role of counsel in any way, it may seek to justify such action by reference to this duty to ensure fair and expeditious proceedings. However, absent any express power contained in procedural rules, there is of course a grey area as to whether a tribunal does indeed have such a power. It is no surprise that this issue has been dealt with very differently by different tribunals and by different national courts.

4.2. Approaches Taken by Tribunals

Only a handful of decisions touch upon this topic of a tribunal's power to remove counsel in the context of international arbitration, and historically the approach by tribunals has been understandably conservative. In an ICC arbitration,[27] the counsel in question had advised the Claimant on its investment into a particular country and

[27] ICC Case No. 8879.

subsequently sought to act for the Respondent in denying the existence of its investment. The arbitral tribunal sitting in Canada held that as this was a dispute outside the scope of the arbitration clause, the matter should be the subject of domestic proceedings, and that any decision of the tribunal to exclude counsel from arbitral proceedings would deprive the relevant party from their right of free choice of counsel and damage the interests of such counsel who is not even bound by an arbitration agreement.

The more recent and best known decisions of tribunals in this area are ICSID decisions. They take a differing approach.

4.2.1. The *Republic of Slovenia* decision[28]

An application was made to the tribunal to exclude an English Queen's Counsel as appearing as advocate, on the basis that the QC practised in the same set of English barristers' chambers as the President of the tribunal. The QC's involvement was only disclosed 10 days before the hearing was due to start.

The tribunal considered whether it had the power to make an order that the Respondent refrain from using the services of the QC in question. The tribunal, having noted that the ICSID Convention and Rules do not "explicitly give the power to tribunals to exclude counsel",[29] found that it had an inherent power to take the necessary measures to preserve the integrity of the proceedings, since Article 44 of the ICSID Convention provided that the tribunal is authorised to decide "any question of procedure" not expressly dealt with in the ICSID Convention, the ICSID Arbitration Rules or "any rule agreed by the parties".[30]

Although the tribunal suggested that a challenge to the President would avoid addressing the question of whether the tribunal had the requisite power, in this situation, since the resignation of the President would have offended the principle of "immutability of Tribunals" (since it was the Respondent who subsequently amended the composition of its legal team "in such a fashion as to imperil the Tribunal's status or legitimacy")[31], an order was made stating that the QC "may not participate further as counsel in this case". It is worth noting that the Claimant asked the tribunal to recommend to the

---

[28] Hrvatska Elektroprivreda, d.d. v. The Republic of Slovenia (ICSID Case No. ARB/05/24), Tribunal's Rule of 6 May 2008, referred to as the *Republic of Slovenia* decision.

[29] *Ibid*, at paragraph 24.

[30] *Ibid*, at paragraph 33.

[31] *Ibid*, at paragraphs 26-28.

Respondent that it "refrain from using the services of the counsel in question at the hearing" only, which raises the question of whether it was within the scope of the tribunal's power to extend this to representation in the entire case.

4.2.2. *Rompetrol v. Romania*[32]

About 18 months after the *Republic of Slovenia* decision, an application was made to an ICSID tribunal to exclude incoming counsel from any involvement in the case because until six months previously he had been a fellow partner of the Claimant's appointee arbitrator. The Respondent decided to challenge the counsel in the arbitration on the basis that the composition of the tribunal was established and uncontested, rather than to challenge the continued functioning of the tribunal or any of its members on the basis that the counsel's participation was "*fait accompli*".[33]

The tribunal in *Rompetrol* took into consideration the fact that the only authority cited for any implied power on the part of the tribunal to control a party's representation was the non-binding *Republic of Slovenia* decision. The tribunal noted the difficulty which any application to exclude counsel faced: "A power on the part of a judicial tribunal of any kind to exercise a control over the representation of the parties in proceedings before it is by definition a weighty instrument, the more so if the proposition is that the control ought to be exercised by excluding or overriding a party's own choice." The tribunal also noted that the existence of a power to exclude counsel would normally be specifically provided for in legal texts and that absent any such express provision, the justification for such a power would be an "overriding and undeniable need to safeguard the essential integrity of the entire arbitral process" and that a control of that kind would be exercised rarely and in compelling circumstances. It stated that if at all, the powers implied in the *Republic of Slovenia* decision would only exist in "extraordinary circumstances, these being circumstances which genuinely touch on the integrity of the arbitral process **as assessed by the Tribunal itself**" (emphasis added).[34]

---

[32] The Rompetrol Group N.V. v. Romania (ICSID Case No. ARB/06/3), Decision of the Tribunal on the Participation of Counsel, 14 January 2010.

[33] *Ibid*, at paragraph 12.

[34] *Ibid*, at paragraphs 15 and 16. It adopted by analogy the test set out in the English House of Lords decision for a tribunal of "whether [a] fair-minded and informed observer, having considered the facts, would conclude that there was a real possibility that the tribunal was biased" (Porter v. Magill [2002] 2 WLR 37, per Lord Hope).

The tribunal in its decision did not seek to exercise this rare power, and thus did not proceed to analyse the scope and extent of such power. It sought to characterise the *Republic of Slovenia* decision as an ad hoc sanction for the failure to make proper disclosure in good time, rather than being a holding of a more general scope. It concluded that the circumstances of the present case did not in any event raise a real possibility of bias and refused to remove counsel.

4.2.3. *Highbury and Ramstein v. Venezuela*[35]

As recently as August 2011, an ICSID tribunal was asked to consider the disqualification of a law firm as counsel to Venezuela based on a perceived conflict of that representation with the firm's other casework in Latin America. The tribunal issued a same-day decision, at the request of the parties, dismissing the challenge.[36]

The arbitral practice on applications relating to the exclusion of counsel is therefore mixed. The *Republic of Slovenia* decision is a rare example of a tribunal's willingness to intervene and to exclude counsel, or at least to limit or circumscribe their role in some way. If a common thread can be discerned, it is that a tribunal may feel able to take measures to limit the role of counsel in exceptional circumstances to safeguard the integrity of the proceedings and the tribunal, but only if that objective cannot be achieved in any other way (for example through the intervention of a bar association).

4.3. Approaches Taken by National Courts

There are also court decisions which have considered this question—and again, there is no clear answer.

It seems that an English court will intervene in respect of English lawyers appearing in English seated arbitrations. In *Koch Shipping Inc v. Richards Butler (A firm)*,[37] an English lawyer acted for the claimant in an arbitration and subsequently moved across to the firm acting for the opponent whilst the arbitration was ongoing. The English court was required to consider an application for an injunction restraining the opponent's law firm (RB) from acting in the London seated arbitration. The English Commercial Court at first instance granted an injunction on the basis that there was a real risk of disclosure of confidential

---

[35] Highbury International AVV and Ramstein Trading Inc. v. Bolivarian Republic of Venezuela (ICSID Case No. ARB/11/1), Decision dated 10 August 2011.

[36] *See,* Global Arbitration Review, Sebastian Perry, *ICSID Panel Declines to Disqualify Counsel,* 15 August 2011.

[37] [2003] C.P. Rep. 10.

information of the solicitor in question; however, this decision was reversed on appeal and the injunction discharged. Both the Commercial Court and Court of Appeal assumed jurisdiction to consider the removal or exclusion of the law firm, RB, acting in the arbitration. It is not known whether the tribunal was first asked to act, but there appeared to be no imminent threat to the integrity of the proceedings. There is also the more recent case of *Gus Consulting v. Leboeuf Lamb Greene & Macrae,* [38] where an arbitration lawyer, an English QC, had moved from another firm to the Respondent law firm, together with colleagues. He took with him a continuing instruction in an arbitration to act for another party against the Claimant. The arbitration was seated in London. The Claimant applied to the English court to exclude his new firm from appearing in the arbitration on the basis that the firm had previously advised it in respect of transactions that were put in issue to some extent in the arbitration. Again, the Court assumed jurisdiction to consider the question of exclusion of counsel, although on the facts it declined to remove or exclude counsel.

It is possible that the assumption of jurisdiction by the English courts in the above examples was on the twin basis that the seat of the arbitration in question in both cases was London and the question concerned English qualified lawyers. It is not clear that the English Court would intervene if the question arose in respect of English lawyers appearing in an arbitration outside of England or in respect of a foreign lawyer appearing in the English-seated arbitration.

Unlike the practice in England and Wales, US court practice appears to be mixed. Following an influential decision of the New York Supreme Court in *Bidermann Industries Licensing v. Avmar* in 1990,[39] some courts have held that the issue of attorney disqualification is best left in the hands of the courts.[40] In *Bidermann,* the Supreme

---

[38] (2006) EWCA 683.

[39] Bidermann Industries Licensing Inc. v. Avmar N.V., N.Y.L.J., Oct. 26, 1990, at 23 (N.Y. Supreme Court, Appellate Division, First Department). The case, involving a dispute concerning certain licensing agreements, concerned an application for disqualification of the Respondents' attorneys from representation in the arbitration proceedings on the ground that the attorneys ought to be called as witnesses due to their involvement in the underlying events and that they received the confidential information of one of the Respondents in the course of representing him in a related earlier transaction. The issue to consider was whether the matter of attorney disqualification could be determined in an arbitration or whether it was a matter exclusively within the province and jurisdiction of the courts. Although remarking that no New York case specifically precluded the arbitration of attorney disqualification issues, the Supreme Court stated that a number of cases imply that attorney conduct is the exclusive province of the courts.

[40] A New York state court concluded in Matter of the Interpublic Group of Cos. v. Trygg (2000) that an application sought to "disqualify an attorney by reason of alleged

Court stayed an arbitration in order to decide an application to remove counsel from the arbitration. It was held that issues of attorney disqualification (1) were intertwined with overriding public policy considerations and could not be left to a tribunal; and (2) involved an application of the Code of Professional Responsibility and the client's constitutional right to choose.

However, other US courts have not so easily assumed jurisdiction. In the case of *Pour le Bebe, Inc. v. Guess? Inc.*[41] the Court of Appeal of California denied an application for challenging an arbitral award on the basis that the counsel's motion for disqualification was refused by the arbitral tribunal for reasons of "corruption, fraud or other due means", and stated in that context that it lacked the power to adjudicate the dispute as Pour Le Bebe's "sole remedy was to obtain relief from the arbitrators". Separately, the US District Court for the Northern District of California held in the case of *Concat LP v. Unilever, Plc*[42] that it could grant the plaintiff's motion for disqualification of the defendant's counsel in the pending litigation proceedings for reasons of conflict of interest notwithstanding the Court's decision to stay those litigation proceedings pending an LCIA arbitration in another forum, and in so doing, recognised that its determination of the issue of disqualification "will have no force outside of its jurisdiction and that the International Court of Arbitration will apply its own conflict rules".

---

violations of the canons of ethics involves substantial questions of public policy. Hence, the decision is one for the court rather than the arbitrator." The 2003 case of Merrill Lynch, Pierce, Fenner & Smith, Inc. v. Benjamin (New York Supreme Court, Appellate Division) noted that issues of attorney disqualification "cannot be left to the determination of arbitrators selected by the parties themselves for expertise in the particular industries in which they are engaged".

41 Pour Le Bebe, Inc., v. Guess? Inc., 112 Cal. App.. 4th 810, 15 October 2003. This case involved a dispute submitted to arbitration relating to royalty payments under certain licenses, and included a motion to disqualify counsel for Guess from representation on the ground that counsel's past representation of Pour Le Bebe resulted in disclosure of confidential information substantially related to the issues raised in the arbitration. The tribunal in the arbitration denied the motion for disqualification on the basis of insufficient evidence and ultimately granted a substantive award in favour of Guess, and Pour Le Bebe subsequently applied and appealed to the Court to vacate the arbitration award. The award was challenged in the Courts by virtue of a section in the Code of Civil Procedure which provided that the court is to vacate an arbitration award if, among other things, "[t]he award was procured by corruption, fraud or other undue means".

42 Concat LP and Chelator, LLC v. Unilever N.V., Unilever U.K. Central Resources Ltd., Unilever United States, Inc., and Concopco, Inc., No. C 04-1396 SI., United States District Court, N.D. California, 7 September 2004.

4.4. Powers of Professional Bodies

It is quite logical that a professional conduct breach should be pursued by the bar association of counsel's home jurisdiction (or one of his home jurisdictions if he is multi-qualified). Various professional conduct rules contemplate this possibility by allocating certain powers in this context to the relevant bar association. By way of example, rule 8.5 of the Model Rules of Professional Conduct of the American Bar Association states as follows:

> (a) Disciplinary Authority. A lawyer admitted to practice in this jurisdiction is subject to the disciplinary authority of this jurisdiction, regardless of where the lawyer's conduct occurs. A lawyer not admitted in this jurisdiction is also subject to the disciplinary authority of this jurisdiction if the lawyer provides or offers to provide any legal services in this jurisdiction. A lawyer may be subject to the disciplinary authority of both this jurisdiction and another jurisdiction for the same conduct.

The commentary to rule 8.5 explains the rationale behind such a principle:

> It is longstanding that the conduct of a lawyer admitted to practice in this jurisdiction is subject to the disciplinary authority of this jurisdiction. Extension of the disciplinary authority of this jurisdiction to other lawyers who provide or offer to provide legal services in this jurisdiction is for the protection of the citizens of this jurisdiction.[43]

The investment treaty arbitration of *Foresti v. South Africa*[44] is a good example of this approach. A particular counsel had been withdrawn as a representative of South Africa in the ICSID arbitration proceedings following allegations of bribery and subsequently, a complaint was made to the General Council of the Bar of South Africa about the conduct of the counsel in question and a disciplinary committee was appointed to investigate the allegations.

But of course, where private international arbitration is concerned, a major practical disincentive is that the conduct which is the subject of the breach usually takes place in private and often

---

[43] *See also,* as further examples, the following: Rules of Conduct of The Paris Bar Association, Article 72.7; French Decree No. 91-1197 of 27 November 1991, Regarding Professional Ethics Rules Applicable to Lawyers, Article 184.

[44] Piero Foresti, Laura de Carli and others v. Republic of South Africa (ICSID Case No. ARB(AF)/07/1).

outside of the jurisdiction where the counsel is qualified. Even though in most cases the Home Bar association will have the formal power to act, the ability of that bar association to do so still depends on a complaint being made to it, and on it having sufficient knowledge to act. Even then, it is doubted whether any bar association would intervene to prevent an ongoing alleged breach, rather than acting *ex post facto* to sanction a past breach. In practice this limits the number of cases where the intervention of a bar association is going to be decisive.

4.5. The Sanctions—What Kind of Punishments?

If a tribunal feels that it should act against counsel, what type of order might it make? There is uncertainty here as well. Most arbitral procedural rules do not at present address this question expressly, although certain institutions are considering amending their rules to make such express provision. However, many arbitral rules do confer upon the tribunal the power to impose such sanctions as it thinks fit by way of interim relief. For example, Article 28 of the ICC Rules gives a tribunal the power to "order any interim or conservatory measure it deems appropriate".

In so far as there is discernible practice in this area, an applicant might seek removal of the advocate from the hearing, or a complete prohibition on representing the client in the matter (which was the outcome in the *Republic of Slovenia* decision), although the latter approach has been the subject of some criticism.[45] There is also a question as to whether costs sanctions can be imposed in such a situation. Any such sanctions would, subject to the terms of the arbitration agreement, likely only be against the parties to the arbitration rather than the counsel acting for them,[46] possibly with a recommendation that such costs are paid by counsel.

5. A WAY OUT?

Having put our thoughts on paper, we conclude that this is an area where there are more questions than answers and this is unlikely to change in the near future. While there are some encouraging initiatives towards a uniform and effective international system that can cater to the world of international arbitration, this will naturally take some time and patience.

---

45 *See, for example,* paragraph 24 of Rompetrol v. Romania.

46 *See,* Chem Asia 2000 Pte. Ltd. v. Oceana Petrochemical AG. 373 F. Supp.2d 340, 356-57 (S.D.N.Y. 2005).

In the meantime, as suggested above, arbitral tribunals may well feel that a sufficiently strong implied power to take action in respect of the conduct of counsel can be constructed, albeit that such power should only be exercised in extreme cases. The *Republic of Slovenia* and *Rompetrol* decisions in particular show that tribunals will continue to take different views as to the scope of such a power, even if they are prepared to imply one.

PART III

Advocacy Training

Advocacy Training for International Commercial and Investment Arbitration[1]

Jeffrey Waincymer

1. INTRODUCTION

A paper dealing with advocacy training for international arbitration should seek to resolve some conceptual tensions before it can set out any meaningful practical blueprint. These tensions involve a consideration of the essential nature of advocacy, which in turn may be affected by differences in procedural and evidentiary approaches to adjudication between key legal families. These differences have led to differences in legal education, both in terms of curriculum and pedagogy, and hence the way graduates approach contentious cases.

At the extreme, to some civilian scholars and practitioners, advocacy as a legal skill is seen as more relevant to the common law oral tradition and its bifurcated profession, where contentious legal work is divided between solicitors and barristers. Even within the common law world, advocacy is too often seen as the exclusive preserve of the barrister class, best learnt on the job via pupilage and experience. Conversely, a civilian lawyer's key role might be suggested as being to understand the scientific theory underlying the relevant law, muster the appropriate evidence and assist an inquisitory adjudicator who would frame the process as best as possible within a broad discretion.

This article seeks to argue against these extremes. It argues that neither extreme view gives appropriate deference to the essential nature of advocacy as persuasion; neither is relevant for modern adjudication in any legal system; and both are certainly inappropriate for international arbitral practice.

The article first looks at the nature of advocacy; differences among legal families as to evidence and procedure that may impact on advocacy skills; then considers the key elements of advocacy; considers teaching options and finishes with a practical training blueprint, outlining the key elements of a training model for law firm and university training.

[1] I would like to acknowledge the invaluable assistance of Alex Fawke in the research and development of this chapter.

2. THE NATURE OF ADVOCACY

It is necessary to first consider what we mean when we talk about advocacy. To advocate a position in an adjudicatory context is to seek to convince the adjudicator of the relative merits of that position. Essentially, advocacy is *persuasion*, involving doing everything necessary to persuade the tribunal to do what you want it to do.[2] A couple of comments can be made about this at the outset.

The most crucial observation in that context, is that it should be a seamless and integrated process, encompassing all steps in an adjudicatory exercise and being of primary concern to all members of a common legal team. The client wants its lawyer to ultimately be successful, meaning that the lawyer will have successfully persuaded the adjudicator. Every activity should be engaged in with that central goal in mind. Other goals, such as a cost effective process, are generally ancillary, no matter how important.

When seen in the above manner, it becomes immediately apparent that advocacy is not simply learning to speak in an eloquent manner at an oral hearing. If the aim is to persuade, then there ought to be a strategy of persuasion adopted throughout. As Pierre-Yves Tschanz has noted, "[t]he arbitrators must think that the case is good, not that counsel is brilliant."[3]

In order to be convincing enough to win any case, counsel must have a *strategy* or *case theory*, i.e., what points do I need to win to get the Award or Order? And why do I need them to get the Award or Order? This tells you which arguments you need to run and where your research efforts are best needed, both as to law and facts.

The second key observation is that, persuasion, like any dynamic communication activity, must be focused on the communicatee, ie, what will best convince the adjudicator given their legitimate and personal known and predicted concerns? Because adjudicators differ, one style cannot fit all. Advocacy is therefore about the utilisation of dynamic skills on a case by case basis.

Thirdly, it must be stressed that, because advocacy describes such a broad range of activities aimed at a broad range of persons, it requires a broad set of skills. Being a good advocate means being a good lawyer in all respects.

---

[2] For further definitions, *see* DAVID ROSS QC, ADVOCACY 1 (2nd ed., 2007); IAIN MORELY, THE DEVIL'S ADVOCATE: A SHORT POLEMIC ON HOW TO BE SERIOUSLY GOOD IN COURT 6 (2nd ed., 2009).

[3] Pierre-Yves Tschanz, *Advocacy in International Commercial Arbitration: Switzerland, in* THE ART OF ADVOCACY IN INTERNATIONAL ARBITRATION, 195, 205 (R Doak Bishop ed.).

A critic of these observations might ask: does advocacy really *matter*? It might be said by such a critic that good arguments will speak for themselves and be obvious to any tribunal. If this is true, the work of the lawyer should not matter—cases are won or lost on their own, self-evident merits.

Experience and logic tell us that this is not true. While the advocate's job is made easier by a strong case, hard work is always required to generate and present the case, in complex matters at least. In most situations where a negotiated settlement cannot be reached easily, the case is likely to be so complicated that the "right" outcome is not self-evident. Moreover, most arbitrators do not have the time (or patience) to develop arguments for each party. They are greatly assisted when the parties can perform this function themselves.[4] For this reason, good advocacy skills are crucial.

Finally, non-arbitration lawyers might wonder whether there is any difference between advocacy in domestic or international litigation and advocacy in international arbitration. This article proceeds on the assumption that many of the advocacy skills which are or ought to be important in national courts are also important in international commercial arbitration. However, there are undoubtedly some important differences that even the best domestic practitioners have to take into account, particularly as a result of the international nature of the process and the need to find common norms or make key choices when parties come from different legal families.[5] To give some obvious examples, a common law lawyer may find that his or her written advocacy skills are tested more rigorously in international arbitration than in domestic litigation and that some habits in oral submissions are frowned upon by arbitral tribunals.[6] So, too, a civilian lawyer might discover that he or she has to develop new skills in examining witnesses and answering questions from the tribunal, which aren't so important in his or her home country. Both may have little experience in arguing about the applicable law or selecting or challenging arbitrators. Because of this, even experienced domestic practitioners would be wise to take time to consider the advocacy skills specific to international arbitration before leaping into practice.

---

4 *See,* R. Doak Bishop, *Toward a Harmonized Approach to Advocacy in International Arbitration, in* THE ART OF ADVOCACY IN INTERNATIONAL ARBITRATION, 451, 452 (R Doak Bishop ed.)

5 *See,* Celeste Hammond and Jeffrey J. Mayer, *Arbitration Advocacy: From Clause to Hearing* 28 AMERICAN JOURNEY OF TRIAL ADVOCACY 101, 102-103 (2004).

6 R. Doak Bishop, *Effective Advocacy in International Arbitration,* METROPOLITAN CORPORATE COUNSEL 25 (May 2005).

3. ARBITRATION ADVOCACY AND DIFFERENCES IN PROCEDURE AND EVIDENCE AMONG LEGAL FAMILIES

There are undoubtedly significant differences in advocacy practice across different countries and legal systems. Where arbitration is concerned, the key differences are more evidentiary than procedural. Because mandatory norms of most *lex arbitri* provide for each party to be given an adequate opportunity to present its case, even civilian trained arbitrators are not unduly inquisitorial.

The key differences are in relation to oral versus documentary evidence; access to documentary evidence; competent witnesses and the respective roles of parties and adjudicator. These can often be explained by cultural differences and variations in legal procedure, evidentiary norms and history.

Because this article concerns advocacy in *international* arbitration, the topic naturally invites a more in depth comparison and discussion of these differences. We will also consider whether there are common optimal norms and how this all impacts upon the art of persuasion. Brief comments are made in this section, with more detailed analysis in the context of advocacy best practice dealt with in the following section, where each stage of the process is separately analysed.

Where oral evidence is concerned, the common law has a long history of jury trials which are usually unknown in civilian systems. When the jury system began, many jurors could not read, and so courts focussed on oral advocacy and minimised written submissions. Because of the concern with lying, great reliance was placed on the cross-examination stage as the testing ground for witness veracity.

Both systems have a certain appeal. It does stand to reason that, by seeing a witness respond to questions in person, we might be able to discern more about the truth of their statements. Advantages include the ability to explore points and have a nuanced discussion. On the other hand, when taken to extremes, some cross-examinations are deliberately rhetorical or argumentative, pore over unimportant subject matter, and can unfairly make genuine witnesses appear untrustworthy. Other disadvantages include the expense and the ability of more eloquent witnesses to be unduly persuasive. Such a process can also advantage articulate liars over less sophisticated but truthful witnesses.

In contrast, civilian cases were heard by educated judges and tended to rely on documents more heavily, on the basis that contemporaneous evidence seems more reliable and because of a greater scepticism as to the ability to determine witness veracity. As Baum has phrased it, civilian courts have traditionally treated oral evidence with "far less importance, if not outright scepticism".[7] This has meant that common law advocates are usually trained in the examination of witnesses, while this may be foreign for many civilian lawyers. Conversely, common lawyers have less practice at persuasive writing.

More contentious is the approach to fact-finding and inferences from facts. It has been suggested that common law lawyers focus more on a rigorous examination of the facts of the case, while civilian lawyers may concentrate more on a scientific analysis of the law and legal policy.[8] The more inquisitorial style might encourage lawyers to wait for adjudicatory guidance in generating the key facts. Even entire legal questions may be left for civilian judges under the doctrine of *iura novit curia*.[9]

Another point at which the two systems differ is in collating the documentary evidence. Common law lawyers expect the opposing party to produce all relevant documents for inspection through the discovery process. It is an important part of the advocate's job to elicit and analyse all of the documents produced and, if this is not done, to seek an order requiring it. By contrast, judges in civilian systems will not automatically require one side to produce additional evidence.[10]

Both approaches have understandable rationales. On the one hand, if relevant evidence exists, it seems like it is in the interests of justice for it to be produced in the pursuit of truth. On the other hand, a defendant might reasonably claim that it should not have to do anything to assist the claimant that has chosen to invade its liberty, presumably on tenable grounds. If the grounds are indeed tenable, the claimant should have had sufficient evidence before it decided to initiate the claim.

The systems also differ in their use of expert witnesses. The common law approach is for the parties to appoint their own experts, while civilian systems tend to rely on court-appointed experts.

Again, both approaches have some appeal. If a party can find an expert that supports its side of the case, it would seem unfair not to allow it that evidence to be heard. On the other hand, there is the potential for a party-appointed expert to be biased, and a court-appointed expert seems like a more neutral and reliable option. Even

---

7 Baum, *International Arbitration: The Path towards Uniform Procedures*, 53.

8 *See*, Doak Bishop, *Towards a Harmonized Approach to Advocacy in International Arbitration*, 454-456.

9 *See*, J. Waincymer, *International Arbitration and the Duty to Know the Law*, JOURNAL OF INTERNATIONAL ARBITRATION 28 no. 3 , 201 (2011).

10 Baum, *International Arbitration: The Path towards Uniform Procedure*, 53.

truthful party appointed experts that differ as to their testimony require a mechanism by which a non-expert tribunal can resolve the differences.

While these are important differences generally and also in the context of advocacy and the processes of developing case strategies, this article argues that the suggested differences are too often exaggerated. There are several reasons for this.

First, common law and civilian law systems are often discussed as if the distinction is pure and obvious. This is misleading. No legal system is purely common law or purely civilian. Over time, both systems have begun to borrow from each other and exchange ideas. Common law and civilian systems now also vary greatly amongst themselves.[11] So the distinction between the two systems is narrowing. This is understandable from a policy perspective. Each is trying to promote optimally fair and efficient dispute resolution processes. Because it is often difficult to maximise both fairness and efficiency without compromise and because policy makers in different cultures might naturally make differing trade-offs, it can be presumed that all systems seek to gravitate towards common ideals from at times differing starting positions.

Secondly, any single proceeding in a common law country may be more "inquisitorial" than a proceeding in a civilian system. Much depends on the facts of the case, the parties and the disposition of the adjudicator. The difference often lies more in tactics and personal style than the legal system in which the parties are operating. James Crawford has noted, in a similar vein, that "even two parties from civil law backgrounds, represented by European lawyers, will usually present their cases in a thoroughly adversarial way."[12]

Finally, in international arbitration, we can now say that some steps have been taken towards a harmonisation of approaches.[13] The most important step was probably the publication and increasing use of the IBA Rules on the Taking of Evidence, now recently revised.[14]

The two key points to be drawn from the foregoing analysis in the context of this article are first, that there is a convergence of norms and second, that advocacy as persuasion must consider how to present the most persuasive factual record in the context of these differing

---

[11] GARY D. BORN, INTERNATIONAL COMMERCIAL ARBITRATION, THIRD EDITION, 1789.

[12] James Crawford, *Advocacy before the International Court of Justice and Other International Tribunals in State-to-State Cases,* in R. DOAK BISHOP, 11-38, 31.

[13] *See,* Born, 1790.

[14] *See,* Axel H. Baum, *International Arbitration: The Path towards Uniform Procedures, in* LIBER AMICORUM IN HONOR OF ROBERT BRINER, 51-61, 56.

evidentiary perspectives, which can impact upon the case strategy that is developed in each case. Differences are still important and impact upon the discretionary decision making of arbitrators concerned to be seen as neutral. The relevance of these differences in the context of specific stages of advocacy planning is explored further in the following section.

4. ARBITRATION ADVOCACY GENERALLY AND THE STAGES OF THE PROCESS

Because of the differences between legal systems noted above, advocacy strategies must be framed within the particular evidentiary system that is operative. Arbitration leaves many such questions to the discretion of the arbitrator, so this is harder to identify with certainty at the outset, although trends in arbitration and the inclinations of proposed and selected arbitrators will be highly relevant. This reminds us that persuasion must be directed at the attributes of the decision-maker and as a result, it must first be emphasised that there is no single model of advocacy that is universally preferred in international arbitration. Naturally, different arbitrators have different preferences and attitudes and, where these are known, advocates should adapt their conduct accordingly.

These differences arise at all stages of a proceeding. At all times, persuasion must be uppermost in a lawyers' mind. Professor George Hampel, a former Australian judge and now full-time advocacy instructor, breaks up the advocate's role into three stages.[15] First, the advocate must engage in rigorous preparation of the case. Only after this can the advocate move on to the next aspect: determining what to submit to the arbitrators in the lead up to and during the hearing. Finally, a good advocate will consider the manner in which the case is communicated. The remainder of this section is separated into all aspects of advocacy from the earliest to the latest stages. Each is addressed in turn. Where arbitration is concerned, it is also useful to explain why strategy can be considered even earlier.

4.1. Drafting Arbitration Agreements and Subsequent Procedural Agreements

In terms of advocacy skills, each lawyer must always ask; what must I prove; by what evidence will I be likely to prove it; how am I to obtain that evidence? An advocacy strategy can even begin at the stage

---

[15] GEORGE HAMPEL QC, ELIZABETH BRIMER AND RANDALL KUNE, ADVOCACY MANUAL: THE COMPLETE GUIDE TO PERSUASIVE ADVOCACY (2008).

of drafting an arbitration agreement, if for example, the agreement calls for utilisation of the IBA Rules or similar evidentiary norms.

4.2. Mastering the Facts and the Law

Even the best advocates are of little use without an understanding of the facts and the law relevant to the case. Mastering these is the first step in any proceeding.

In international arbitrations, unlike domestic litigation, mastering the law does not simply mean finding the appropriate statute or case. There can, of course, be disputes as to which law is applicable, and this can be crucial in determining the outcome of the case.[16] An advocate needs to be persuasive as the methodologies available for choice of law issues, whether conflicts approaches or approaches based on identified implied choice of the parties. Such choice of law issues can also impact upon choice of arbitrator. Mastering the facts requires consideration of the fact finding issues referred to above. An optimal persuasion strategy will need to factor in the way evidence is admitted and evaluated by any tribunal.

4.3. Developing a Case Theory

Developing a good case theory or strategy is the most crucial step in any arbitration or litigation. It is worth expanding on this notion in some detail. A case theory is the central theme or points that need to be presented to convince the tribunal to make an order in your favour. It can only be developed after a thorough analysis of the facts and law and a consideration of the way an arbitral tribunal is likely to handle contentious questions.

Before the case theory is established, the advocate cannot prepare more specific aspects of the case, such as statements at the hearing, examination of witnesses and written submissions.[17] The case theory guides and informs all of these, and so is an important early step for the advocate to take. It should be considered as early as possible as it guides research, choice of evidence and submission focus. Once again, the essential thesis of this article is that on this basis, advocacy has to be seen as a seamless aspect of the entire adversarial process.

Once a case strategy is developed, other choices can be made. For example, a weak argument that is *essential* for that goal must be

---

[16] *See,* Doak Bishop, *Towards a Harmonized Approach to Advocacy in International Arbitration*, above n. 3, 455.

[17] Hampel Brimer and Kune, above n. 6, 33.

prepared and presented as strongly as possible. A weak *alternative* argument might be dropped or presented briefly. This can be particularly important where there are clear time constraints, such as under chess clock arbitration.

A key element of the case strategy is to consider what factual record to present, including how best to undermine the factual contentions of the other side. Meticulous analysis of the facts and law are required, as well as an ability to present them clearly. Before this, an appropriate factual record must be generated, being an amalgam of witness testimony, party and third party documents and identification of the inferences and conclusions of fact that might be drawn from such a record.

Differences in dispute settlement norms between legal families impact this element, both as to the procedure by which case strategies are presented and as to the admissibility and access to evidence, whether of parties, experts or documents held by the opposing party. This is dealt with in the following sub-sections.

While these differences may impact upon advocacy strategies, in all cases an advocate is essentially trying to tell a *compelling* story that will hopefully equate strongly with the final award. Because of this, the structure of written and oral submissions should largely follow an ideal award order. For example, when making final submissions at the hearing, or dealing with sequential written submissions, the person speaking or writing first can do this easily. The person responding has to marry this aim with a separate goal of conveying the impression that they are truly responsive to their opponents' arguments, ie try to present your coherent respondent theory and also negate the claimant's key points in a seamless integrated fashion. If the respondent just presents its theory, it sounds like it has not engaged or responded. If it just attacks claimant's arguments one by one, there is no overall theory and the ambience is too defensive. Conversely, the claimant aims to deal so comprehensively with respondent's key arguments in advance, that the respondent will sound unpersuasive, having lost the ability to get any immediate sympathy. As noted, where written submissions are concerned, the above model works naturally when they are directed to be sequential. On the other hand, when they are simultaneous, each must aim to be pre-emptive as to arguments that ought to be anticipated from the other side.

As mentioned, the overall aim of advocacy is to *persuade* the adjudicator. In order to do so, in my view, your aim is to be seen as a *trustworthy*, and *convincing expert*.

To be *expert* means having and displaying all pertinent knowledge of facts and law as and when needed, but not giving a lecture for its own sake either in written or oral submissions.

To be *trustworthy* means that the adjudicator trusts you to address all relevant aspects of the argument, law and facts, both those favourable and also those which your opponent will suggest are unfavourable to your case. You generally only believe someone when you can trust that they are not misrepresenting the strengths of their case or glossing over key aspects of it. You still seek to show why the purportedly unfavourable aspects of your case are not determinative, but the adjudicator should at least feel that they do not need to distrust you or at least check up on you.[18] Nothing undermines credibility with arbitrators faster than misleading them. When counsel presents the case in an exaggerated manner, the arbitrators' reasoning tends to be as follows: this counsel has presented certain aspects of the case in a biased way. Therefore, the overall story that he or she is asking me to believe must be distorted.[19] To create such scepticism does a great disservice to the client.

As part of not overstating their case, advocates should be careful in their choice of words. It is tempting to use words like "clearly" and "obviously" in both written and oral submissions. Such language is not only superfluous. It is also risky. Often, the point being made will be far from clear or obvious to the other party or the tribunal.[20] This can easily attract critical comments or questions from the arbitrators.

To be *convincing*, means you present a compelling set of reasons why your position should be the preferred one. This covers both substance and presentation.

So what makes something seem sensible and convincing? In other words, what distinguishes a good case theory from a bad one? In my view, to be convincing, you are ideally trying to appeal to "gut", "heart" and "head" all at the same time.

By "gut" I mean the intuitive first blush look at a problem (ie the gut reaction). What is the immediate reaction that you think the adjudicator will take and how might you favourably influence this? In this way you try and have the adjudicator on side as early as possible. It is easier to *reinforce* a favourable preliminary view taken by the adjudicator than *change* an unfavourable one. This makes you think about the type of opening remarks that will get the tribunal onside

---

[18] R. Doak Bishop, *Advocacy from the Arbitrator's Perspective, in* THE ART OF ADVOCACY IN INTERNATIONAL ARBITRATION, 442 (R. Doak Bishop ed.).

[19] Tschanz, *Advocacy in International Commercial Arbitration: Switzerland*, 206.

[20] Tschanz, *Advocacy in International Commercial Arbitration: Switzerland*, 206.

from the outset, if possible. Written submissions will also have concentrated on this. Ideally the Notice of Arbitration and Statement of Claim will have done so already.

By "heart" I mean appeals for sympathy and appeals to notions of fairness. An important aspect of the case theory is the human sense of fairness or, as Doak Bishop has phrased it, the "equities" of the case.[21] Winning a technical logical argument is not always enough. The arbitrators need to be convinced that, deep down, you are in the right[22] and that their decision will be seen as just.

By "head" I mean the legal logic of the argument. While it will not always be determinative when equity issues point in different directions, many arbitrators are primarily concerned with a justifiable scientific logic that does not make them seem overly adventurous as adjudicators. Where issues of legal doctrine or conflicting technical facts are involved, a convincing argument will have well thought out logical reasoning as a key element.

If we put these all together it means that an optimal argument (and any advocacy) will not only be sound in terms of legal authority but it will be well reasoned, logical, commercially desirable and sensible to a practical arbitrator and hopefully business people who would observe the outcome, morally reasonable and will be an argument that the Tribunal will think it will be respected for when included in the award. This applies to written and oral submissions and also applies to answers to questions.

Good arguments also need to be understood and communication skills are vital. Good communication also means being clear, precise and as concrete as possible.[23] Advocates should say exactly what they mean and avoid being vague. This is essential for the arbitrators to understand and accept your case. If your argument is not clear, it is unlikely to form part of the award rendered by the tribunal. Some arbitrators may even suspect that an unclear argument is deliberately vague to hide its weakness. To achieve clarity and precision, it is important to use simple language and short sentences. Language issues are important, with many arbitrators hearing cases in other than their native language.

While competent arbitrators should be concerned with the merits and not theatrics, they are human and effective communication must be engaging. International arbitrators are busy (and often jet-lagged). Keeping them interested in the case is an important aspect of

---

21 *See,* Doak Bishop, *Effective Advocacy in International Arbitration,* above n. 3, 25.

22 *See* , Tschanz, above n. 2, 206.

23 R. DOAK BISHOP, ADVOCACY FROM THE ARBITRATORS' PERSPECTIVE, 443.

advocacy.[24] To do this, counsel has to project a sense of enthusiasm and a belief that the case deserves close attention and concentration. The arbitrators are unlikely to be interested in a case which counsel does not appear to be interested in. If the oral advocacy is uninteresting, the tribunal might simply wait for its own careful reflection on written material to make the final determination.

4.4. Selecting Arbitrators

If persuasion needs to be considered at all stages, then this can even encompass selection of a tribunal. A major difference between domestic litigation and arbitration is the ability for parties, in some cases, to select the arbitrators. Choosing an appropriate or inappropriate arbitrator influences the running of the arbitration and, potentially, the outcome.[25] As such, selecting the right arbitrator is an important part of advocacy in arbitration.

What should parties look for in a potential arbitrator? It might be thought that the most important quality is a predisposition to a party's side of the case. No doubt, this can be one consideration, and many parties naturally feel more comfortable if one of the arbitrators shares their nationality, legal background or expertise. Further, as Charles J. Moxley Jr. has noted, a party may wish to choose an arbitrator with a reputation as a rule-oriented strict constructionist or a more equity-oriented open-minded arbitrator, depending on the advocate's case.[26] At the very least, parties are well within their rights to ensure that an arbitrator has no predisposition *against* their case. However, a few words of caution are necessary, drawing on an excellent article by R. Doak Bishop on the matter.[27]

There are both legal and practical reasons for not choosing an arbitrator who is obviously predisposed to one side of the case. First, most arbitral rules require arbitrators to be, and appear to be, independent and impartial. Any arbitrator not meeting these requirements can be challenged by the other party and removed. This obviously rules out an arbitrator who has written a specific opinion on the case. But beyond this, it is probably not in a party's interest to choose an arbitrator too favourable to its own side of the case. As Doak

---

[24] *See,* Tschanz, *Advocacy in International Commercial Arbitration: Switzerland,* 207.

[25] *See,* Charles J. Moxley Jr, *Selecting the Ideal Arbitrator,* 60(3) DISPUTE RESOLUTION JOURNAL 24 (2005)

[26] *Ibid,* 26.

[27] *See* , R. Doak Bishop, *Towards a Harmonized Approach to Advocacy in International Arbitration,* above n. 3, 460.

Bishop has noted, arbitrators often bond over their shared impartiality and belief that they are working together to decide the case appropriately.[28] A clearly predisposed arbitrator may not bond with the rest of the panel in this way and, consequently, may have little influence on the other arbitrators. Advocates should be wary of this potential perverse effect. Finally, if there is an incentive for one party to select a more predisposed person, the other party should do likewise, cancelling out any value in the strategy and ensuring a more polarised and possibly less harmonious tribunal.[29]

So rather than looking only to a potential arbitrator's predisposition, a range of other factors should be considered.[30] The arbitrator should be a person of integrity who will not be influenced by inappropriate considerations or pressure. He or she should be intelligent, capable of recognising strong arguments and seeing through weak ones. Expertise in arbitration law or a particular industry is also important, though this depends on the particular facts of the case. Doak Bishop further suggests that the arbitrator should be articulate and have a personality that will enable him or her to develop a good relationship with the parties and other members of the tribunal.[31]

4.5. Documentary Evidence

Evidentiary strategies and the desirability of trustworthiness can depend upon the duty to provide adverse documents and the ability to obtain favourable documents from the opposing party. As noted, legal families differ significantly on these issues.

To the extent that any trend is discernible in international arbitration, it is worth noting that Article 3 of the IBA Rules on Taking Evidence requires parties to submit all relevant documents to the tribunal. A party can also make a "request to produce", requiring the other side to produce specific documents or "a narrow and specified requested category of documents". We might tentatively say, then, that the logic behind the discovery process is becoming more widely

---

28 *Ibid.*

29 Even where this is accepted, it is a classic Prisoners Dilemma where each will adopt the sub-optimal strategy knowing they will be better off if the other side does not do likewise, for fear that the converse will occur where they do not.

30 *Ibid.*

31 *Ibid.*

accepted.[32] Open ended fishing expeditions are not supported, but this is the case with emerging common litigation practice as well.

From an advocacy as persuasion perspective, the difference means that under civilian norms, an optimal strategy should see the claimant with a sufficient evidentiary record at the outset. A common law approach can hope to generate parts of that record through the document production processes.

4.6. Written Submissions

The exact procedure of the written submissions in an international arbitration will depend on the arbitral rules and scheduling order of the arbitrator.[33] But in most international arbitrations, written submissions are a substantial and important part of the advocates' role. For some common lawyers, the notion of written advocacy is not well understood. In the United States, for example, advocacy in written submissions is almost unknown, because the jury does not see them.[34] But in international arbitrations, written submissions are crucial, as they provide the first opportunity to persuade the tribunal. And, as psychological studies of American juries have shown, first impressions matter—probably more than they should.[35]A few brief, general comments can be made about good written advocacy.

Written submissions are more permanent and enduring than oral submissions. Because of this, advocates should be careful to avoid inconsistency. Once written submissions have been made, counsel should be cautious not to drastically change his or her story, which can, of course, undermine credibility.[36]

---

32 *See,* SIEGFRIED ELSING AND JOHN TOWNSEND, .BRIDGING THE COMMON LAW-CIVIL LAW DIVIDE.

33 Doak Bishop, *Towards a Harmonized Approach to Advocacy in International Arbitration,* above n. 3, 468.

34 Doak Bishop, *Effective Advocacy in International Arbitration,* above n. 5, p. 25. Note that this is changing in some common law jurisdictions. In Australia, for example, written submissions have become far more common in the past 25 years. *See,* Justice JD Heydon, *Aspects of Rhetoric in Forensic Advocacy Oveer the Past 50 Years, in* REDISCOVERING RHETORIC: LAW, LANGUAGE AND THE PRACTICE OF PERSUASION, 217, 231-134 (Justin Gleeson and Ruth Higgins eds.).

35 Doak Bishop, *Towards a Harmonized Approach to Advocacy in International Arbitration,* above .n 3, 470.

36 Doak Bishop, *Towards a Harmonized Approach to Advocacy in International Arbitration,* above n. 3, 469.

As far as writing style is concerned, advocates obviously need to be clear, concise and accurate.[37] Beyond this, a delicate balance must be maintained. On the one hand, written submissions must be interesting enough to maintain the reader's attention, but not too flashy and combative. Confrontational or sarcastic comments are not only unlikely to influence the final award,[38] they can also be offensive to some arbitrators (perhaps especially those with civil law backgrounds).[39] On the other hand, written submissions must be sufficiently academic in discussing the law to convey necessary complexities and detail, but should not be so abstruse and dense as to put the reader to sleep. In considering their writing style, foreign advocates might find it useful to consult one of the numerous books available on writing in English if that is the language of the arbitration.[40]

Finally, unlike litigation in some national courts, all important points should be included in written submissions.[41] Counsel should not save up what he or she perceives to be spectacular surprises for the oral hearings. This might be effective in front of a jury, but is unlikely to impress time-poor international arbitrators.

4.7. Opening Statements

The opening statement, if allowed for, provides another important opportunity to make a strong early impression on the tribunal.[42] Although it is designed to make a good first impression, it should be one of the final things worked on by the advocate. It is not until counsel has a clear idea of how to present the entire case that the opening statement should be developed.[43]

What should be included in an opening statement? Essentially, an opening statement should amount to two things: a summary and a

---

37 *See,* Justice Kenneth Hayne, *Written Advocacy* (Paper presented as part of the continuing legal education program of the Victorian Bar, 5 and 26 March 2007) 5.

38 Tschanz, *Advocacy in International Commercial Arbitration: Switzerland,* 216.

39 Doak Bishop, *Towards a Harmonized Approach to Advocacy in International Arbitration,* above n. 3, 472.

40 *See,* Justice Kenneth Hayne, *Written Advocacy,* above n. 20, 2. Justice Hayne cites as good starting texts: Strunk and White's *The Elements of Style, Fowlers' Modern English Usage,* Sir Ernest Gowers' *The Complete Plain Words,* Fowler's *The King's English* and Garner's *The Elements of Legal Style.*

41 Doak Bishop, *Towards a Harmonized Approach to Advocacy in International Arbitration,* above n. 3, 469.

42 Doak Bishop, *Advocacy in International Commercial Arbitration: United States, in* THE ART OF ADVOCACY IN INTERNATIONAL ARBITRATION, 343 (R. Doak Bishop ed.)

43 *See,* Hampel, Brimer and Kune, above n 6, 34.

story.[44] It is a summary, in the sense that it does not need to contain all of the details of the case. The panel only needs to gain an overall view of the case and its direction. The specifics can often be left for witness testimony or written statements.

At the same time, the opening statement should be a story which captures the panel's attention and interest. Like a good story, it should be easy to understand and interesting. It almost goes without saying, however, that it should not be overly dramatic or overstated, which, as discussed, can undermine credibility. This may be especially true in front of arbitrators with civilian law backgrounds, where opening statements are often seen as redundant.[45]

4.8. Examination of Witnesses

The most obvious difference between the two systems probably lies in the examination of witnesses.[46] It is important for advocates in international arbitration to be aware of these differences. As Elsing and Townsend have noted, oral evidence that common law lawyers might assume wins the case for them may be unconvincing to a civil law arbitrator more accustomed to contemporaneous documentary evidence. So, too, civilian lawyers should be conscious of the potential for common law arbitrators to place significant weight on oral evidence.[47]

4.9. Direct Examination of Witnesses

Again with the aim of time efficiency in mind, the examination of the witness should be as brief and concise as possible. Oral evidence is difficult for even the most focussed arbitrators to follow, and this should be kept in mind.

Increasingly, written witness statements are used instead of direct examination of witnesses.[48] However, when direct examination of witnesses is permitted, certain rules should be followed. Doak Bishop emphasises that the written statements of the witness can be used to save the tribunal's time and avoid going over uncontroversial points.[49]

---

[44] *Ibid*, 65-68.

[45] Tschanz, *Advocacy in International Commercial Arbitration: Switzerland*, 217.

[46] Julian Lew and Laurence Shore, *International Commercial Arbitration: Harmonizing Cultural Differences*, 54 DISPUTE RESOLUTION JOURNAL 34 (1999); *see also*, ELSING AND TOWNSEND, BRIDGING THE COMMON LAW-CIVIL LAW DIVIDE.

[47] *See*, ELSING AND TOWNSEND, BRIDGING THE COMMON LAW-CIVIL LAW DIVIDE.

[48] *See*, Doak Bishop, *Towards a Harmonized Approach to Advocacy in International Arbitration*, 480.

[49] Doak Bishop, *Towards a Harmonized Approach to Advocacy*, 481.

Counsel can simply ask the witness to confirm certain aspects of his or her written statement, and save the oral testimony for the most persuasive parts.

If oral testimony has to be long, then the advocate should vary his or her speed and presentation. It can also be helpful to expressly state when a question is important. According to Doak Bishop, Abraham Lincoln used this technique when he was a trial lawyer, prefacing key questions with phrases such as "the next question goes to the key issue in this case and is very important. Please think about it carefully before you answer."[50] Strategies along these lines can be useful for maintaining the arbitrators' attention to the case strategy.

Direct examination can also be an important opportunity to acknowledge and address weaknesses in the case.[51] As discussed above in the context of trustworthiness, being upfront about such vulnerabilities reduces the impact that these weaknesses have when raised by the opposing party.

4.10. Cross-examination of Witnesses

As discussed above, common law trial lawyers tend to be extensively trained in cross-examining witnesses. The common law approach assumes that, through oral examination, we can determine the character and credibility of the witness. It is thus a crucial part of the advocate's role to establish or undermine this credibility. Civilian lawyers, by contrast, often feel uncomfortable about this process.[52] Such examination, if it occurs at all, is normally conducted by judges, not the parties' advocates.[53] The role of the advocate is normally limited to suggesting questions for the judge to ask.[54]

If a harmonised approach is emerging, it is to allow, but limit examination of witnesses by parties. Parties are typically allowed to cross-examine witnesses if they so wish, but effort is made to ensure that these are brief and to the point.[55] In this way, the excesses of the common law trial lawyer are constrained, while still allowing the opportunity to present important evidence orally.[56]

---

50 Doak Bishop, *Towards a Harmonized Approach to Advocacy*, 482.

51 *See*, Kaj Hobér, *Advocacy in International Commercial Arbitration: Sweden*, in R. DOAK BISHOP, THE ART OF ADVOCACY IN INTERNATIONAL ARBITRATION.

52 Lew and Shore, *International Commercial Arbitration: Harmonizing Cultural Differences*, 34.

53 Lew, Mistellis and Kröll, 533-534.

54 ELSING AND TOWNSEND, BRIDGING THE COMMON LAW-CIVIL LAW DIVIDE.

55 Lew and Shore, *International Commercial Arbitration: Harmonizing Cultural Differences*, 35.

56 *See*, ELSING AND TOWNSEND, BRIDGING THE COMMON LAW-CIVIL LAW DIVIDE.

Cross-cultural issues are still relevant as civilian arbitrators may be uncomfortable with common law techniques. Nevertheless there are some well respected principles and various well-known cross-examiners have developed certain rules for cross-examining witnesses. For experts, these rules can probably be ignored in the right circumstances. But for the vast majority of practitioners, following rules such as these will likely go a long way towards improving cross-examination.

Because it is so challenging, much has been written about the "golden rules" of cross-examination. Advocates with little experience in cross-examination would do well to consult these. One list of cross-examination rules, which is preferred by Professor Hampel, comes from the American advocacy teacher Professor Irving Younger's 10.[57] Obviously, these rules do not tell us everything we need to know about successful cross-examination. But they are certainly a good starting point.

(1) Be brief. There are two reasons to do this: The more you do, the more likely you will make an error; and the less the number of key points, the easier they are absorbed, (although the latter point was made in respect of jury trials).

(2) Use short questions and plain words.

(3) Ask only leading questions. Don't ever ask non-leading questions. If you do, the witness will run away with it and you lose control.

(4) Never ask a question to which you do not already know the answer.

(5) Listen to the answer.

(6) Don't quarrel with the witness. If the answer sounds ridiculous, you do not need to point this out and attack the witness.

(7) Don't give the witness the opportunity to repeat their points from examination in chief.

(8) Never permit the witness to explain anything. Witnesses are of course entitled to do this, but it is not the role of cross-examination.

(9) Don't ask the one question too many.

---

57 Hampel, Brimer and Kune, above n. 6, 112-114.

(10) Save the ultimate point for the closing address.

4.11. Expert Witnesses

In international arbitrations, the trend has been to allow both party appointed and tribunal appointed experts. In this way, potentially convincing expert testimony, provided by one of the parties, is not ignored, but there remains an arguably more trustworthy source. The trend is also to utilise witness conferencing to engage the conflicting experts in a discussion that will allow the arbitrator to choose which view to prefer. Persuasion strategies and methods of questioning will obviously differ in each circumstance.

4.12. Closing Statements

Closing statements try and tie it all together and convince the tribunal that counsel did indeed establish the factual and legal contentions needed.

4.13. Language Issues

Because of the global nature of international commercial arbitration, counsel may address arbitrators or witnesses who are not native speakers in the language of the arbitration.

Advocates should not ignore possible language barriers. If the language of the arbitration is foreign to one of the arbitrators, it becomes even more important than usual to be clear and precise, using simple, short sentences. An arbitrator is unlikely to admit during a hearing that he or she did not understand a particular phrase, so the onus is on the advocate to ensure that everything is understood. Advocates should be aware of aspects of their language which are unique to one country and may not be universally understood. Care should also be taken to speak in as neutral an accent as possible, though obviously this should not appear too forced. Colloquialisms and slang phrases should of course be avoided. It is important to remember, however, that many international arbitrators speak several languages with near-native fluency. If an arbitrator is clearly very competent in the language of the arbitration, then the advocate needs to be careful to not simplify his or her speech so much as to appear patronising.

If an interpreter is necessary, the advocate should take a number of steps to ensure that nothing is lost or, perhaps worse, distorted in translation. The first task is to choose an appropriate interpreter. If possible, it is preferable to use a reputable translation agency and an accredited interpreter. Once an interpreter is chosen, it is important to prepare him or her for the hearing.[58] Oral interpreting is difficult, even for those who have a complete mastery of the two languages, and the advocate should keep this in mind. The interpreter must understand in advance any technical or unusual terms which are likely to be significant at the hearing. It has been suggested that it may be better to have consecutive, rather than simultaneous, interpretation to minimise the chance of confusion.[59]

5. ADVOCACY ISSUES IN LEGAL EDUCATION

If the previous thoughts on the importance of advocacy are valid, the next question is how best to inculcate these skills in law graduates and in law firm trainees.

From a law firm's perspective, it might explore in-house mentoring programs and/or encourage postgraduate specialist training in suitable areas. Companion papers in this volume address some of the latter. I believe that much more could be done by large firms in-house by having skilled educators work with trainees on real matters being conducted by the firm, to enhance their strategic and practical skills. This could take many forms. One example might be regular meetings in seminar style where trainees working on a particular matter report as to the issues and challenges, have other members of the group consider how they would have approached the matter, and have senior staff explain why they have approached the situation in the way they have.

The latter is an important aspect of having young professionals understand the importance of heuristics, ie, the way experts go about certain functions. Often it is extremely difficult to set out an objective formula for the way experts behave, why they follow certain norms in most cases and when and why they think it strategically desirable to take a different tack in a particular case. The educator could work with law firm partners to identify suitable cases for such discussions and try and structure the learning program for the trainees. In very large law firms where trainees sometimes feel dissatisfied in being delegated to do more menial tasks without understanding the overall strategy in an individual matter, this can help enhance their job satisfaction as well as their skills development.

Advocacy training in legal education is more contentious. First, the differences in legal families impact upon the differences in legal

---

58 R. Doak Bishop, *Towards a Harmonized Approach to Advocacy in International Arbitration*, 488.

59 Tschanz, *Advocacy in International Commercial Arbitration: Switzerland*, 220.

education.[60] Historically both common law and civilian legal systems eschewed a skills orientation, although this was more marked where civilian legal education was concerned. There are a number of reasons for this. Because civilian law was primarily concerned to deduce conclusions on specific fact situations from broad codified principles, it was said to be more concerned with a scientific synthesis of principle and a rigorous logic. The common law, relying on *stare decisis,* was more concerned with inductive conclusions from decided cases. The civilian deductive approach could be seen as more akin to higher forms of intellectual analysis on a par with other branches of university thought. Conversely, the common law, drawing inductive conclusions from what actually occurs in cases, had a more necessarily practical orientation,[61] in turn leading to case method as a key form of university teaching.

Nevertheless, while each may have started from differing perspectives, each legal system seeks to resolve the same problems. As a result, legal education ought to cover a similar skills set, albeit in differing ratios.[62] Over time, civilian legal education has incorporated some of the techniques of the common law style such as case method, Socratic questioning and, of most significance to this article, mooting in events such as the Vis Moot. European institutions have also been influential in establishing investment arbitration and World Trade Organisation moots. Such developments have come out of a realisation that expository scientific lectures, important as they may be in terms of the essence of law, can do too much of the work for the student, to the detriment of their intellectual development.[63]

These issues are of even more concern where international issues are concerned. A thoughtful approach to comparative law, both to understand differing cultural norms, draw inspiration for policy conclusions and to understand one of the key influences in arbitral practice, is also a key legal education development.[64] As Klaus Peter

---

[60] M Damaska, *A Continental Lawyer in an American Law School: Trials and Tribulations of Adjustment,* 116 UNIVERSITY OF PENNSYLVANIA LAW REV 1363 (1968); J H Merryman, *Legal Education There and Here: A Comparison,* 27 STANFORD LAW REV 859 (1975).

[61] *See,* Justice Michael Kirby, *Rhetoric in Law—A Case for Optimism?, in* GLEESON AND HIGGINS, REDISCOVERING RHETORIC, above n. 47, 195-196.

[62] C Valcke, *Legal Education in a "Mixed Jurisdiction": The Quebec Experience,* 10 TUL EUR & CIV LR 61 (1995).

[63] J Gordley, *Comparative Law in Legal Education,* 75 TULANE LAW REV 1003, 1013 (2001).

[64] K P Berger, *Harmonisation of European Contract Law: The Influence of Comparative Law,* 50 INTERNATIONAL AND COMPARATIVE LAW QUARTERLY 877 (2001); K P Berger, *Arbitration as a Source of Inspiration for Comparative Law, Legal Teaching and the*

Berger has observed, the "natural comparative orientation and flexible procedural framework" of international arbitration makes it an ideal format in which to consider comparative aspects of legal systems.[65] Thus for arbitration practitioners, a skills oriented advocacy training program should be essential.

6. TRAINING GUIDE TO ADVOCACY PRACTICE

This section sets out some of the key elements of the approach I take to mooting and advocacy training in relation to international commercial arbitration. It essentially occurs in a university environment but would apply equally to law firm training of graduates and mentoring by arbitration practitioners of their support staff.

At the outset, because of the above view of advocacy as seamless persuasion in the context of an optimal case strategy, I see the endeavour as an element of comprehensive practical legal training. Ideally, that involves getting trainee lawyers and students to integrate substantive laws such as contract law, with procedure and evidence, in the simulated context of written and oral advocacy. I believe that this is the best form of legal education, but resources and historical approaches militate against its broad adoption in most law schools around the world. I primarily engage in this process within the context of the Willem C Vis International Commercial Arbitration Moot. The Vis Moot is ideal as it naturally brings together contract issues and arbitral procedure and theory. It is better than other moots for this purpose as it always contains a messy documentary record, with students having to identify contract rights and obligations from debatable but realistic evidence, rather than from stipulated fact situations as found in typical law school examinations.

Turning to the advocacy itself, I seek to highlight the following key points, many of which have been articulated above.

It is important to remember at the outset that, as with any communication activity, there are different styles that are possible, differing theories, and most importantly, differing listener preferences and attributes, so there cannot be one model that is inherently correct for all listeners in all situations.

Nevertheless, there are techniques that are widely accepted and key challenges and strategies that students should always be aware of. Importantly, even though there is no uniform model, counsel still must

---

Transnational Negotiation Process, in BÖCKSTIEGEL K-H, PERSPECTIVES OF AIR LAW, SPACE LAW AND INTERNATIONAL BUSINESS LAW FOR THE NEXT CENTURY, 318 (1995).

65 K P Berger, *op cit*, n. 61.

always think about which advocacy approaches to adopt in any case they are asked to present.

6.1. Moot Advocacy versus "Real" Advocacy

If a practical simulation is attempted in a university environment, it is important to both convince the students of the value of this approach, but also point out any ways in which the simulation may differ from real practice. In this context it is important for them to understand the distinction between *moot* advocacy and real world advocacy. In my view, they differ in a few key respects:

1. Moot judges are asked to assess reasoning, presentation and performance and do not assess the underlying merits of counsel's client's case.
2. The less knowledgeable the moot judge is about the law or the intricacies of the particular moot problem, the more they will tend to count performance and style over substance (I do not concentrate on the latter although I do not ignore it either).
3. In most student moots (including Vis), counsel only has 15-20 minutes (including interruptions) to cover material that would take many hours or in some cases even days in a real case. This is unrealistic when a typical moot problem has a range of issues of fact and law to squeeze into that time-frame, but this is still good training. Learning to be succinct without losing persuasiveness is a key skill. I point out that because of this time constraint, it is not essential that students cover all points in a moot, even though they should strive to do so. This is unlike a real case where you must put all arguments you intend to rely upon, although you would drop weak arguments to save costs and not annoy the adjudicator.
4. In a moot, students often do not have all key facts, yet must still argue each issue. This forces them to discuss some hypothetical fact situations in a way which would never happen in a real hearing. I point out that in a real case, the person with the burden on that issue would lose out if they had not brought evidence forward in support of that issue.
5. If the problem gives one party a weak argument, counsel at least needs to consider running it in a moot lest they be seen as avoiding the set challenge (although some moot judges

suggest the opposite on the basis that it shows good judgment), whereas in the real world you could give it up unless it was essential to you winning. In many moots, the stand-out performers are often the ones with the best ways of handling the weakest points that would not win in a real case no matter how well put. You are being compared to other advocates facing the same challenge and can excel in this way on a comparative basis. (Many judges may not even realise that this is why they are impressed!)

In other respects, the two forms of advocacy are similar. I concentrate on advocacy training for practice and not for winning moot competitions where the two strategies would differ. The following are key extracts from the notes I provide to students and which are the essence of my ongoing engagement with them. Subject to the above caveats, most of the points below are in my view the essence of good real world advocacy.

6.2. The Aims of Advocacy

I first concentrate on:

(1) The nature of advocacy, explaining that it permeates all stages of adjudication.

(2) The nature and importance of a case strategy and the need to appeal to logic and fairness as quickly as possible, discussed above as appeals to head, heart and gut.

I invite students to consider throughout their preparation whether they would be convinced by their own arguments. If not, more development of crucial arguments and/or presentation is needed. This applies to practitioners as well. Too often people just do "busy" work in preparing, without evaluating how convincing the submissions are likely to be and how they might best be improved. Always ask: if you were your own client, would you be happy to pay for the work done? Clients rightly care about results, not hours worked.

6.3. Structuring Your Argument

Arguments should be structured into a logical framework consistent with the case strategy and the award you are ideally hoping to read in due course. There are a number of subsidiary elements:

- *Arguments should normally be introduced by the conclusion you want the tribunal to reach, then the reasoning, then a reiteration of the conclusion.* This is for two reasons. Adjudicators always need to know where you are going. Secondly, it is never too early to appeal to the "gut." Thus in opening every issue, the ideal is to introduce it and if possible, characterise the issues and facts so that you have already begun to convince the adjudicator. This is very tricky because if you present a debatable proposition in such an introduction, an adjudicator might justifiably question you at that stage, which leads to the opposite effect, as you didn't want to start your argument in the middle of your introduction, particularly if you are doing so in a defensive fashion in response to an adjudicator who did not accept your characterisation. So how do we deal with this? In a moot context, we aim to continually work to have about 20 or so key sentences that at least appeal to the gut as introductory remarks and which also double as the basis of your last 3 minutes when you are running out of time. (I ask students to do 5 minute moots every day with no notes so that they practice thinking and talking at the same time and also become comfortable with the unrealistic 20 minute timeframe. If they become comfortable with 5 minutes, 20 minutes feels like a luxury. In any event, I point out that if they haven't come up with an idea that convinces in 5 minutes, they probably haven't developed a good argument as yet.)

- On the one hand I am trying to train students to squeeze hours of submissions into 20 minutes. Again, it is the key sentences that state it all succinctly and convincingly that we try and develop and work on more and more as we get closer to the formal moot. On the other hand we are eventually brave and strategic in selecting which arguments to run and which not to run. That is most important in practice when clients don't want to pay for long, weak arguments. What I don't want students to do is drop apparently weak arguments before they have developed them as well as can be. Experienced lawyers may do so but as students, exploring all possible arguments is the best way to develop innovative thinking and evaluative skills. Also, given that students are developing advocacy skills at the same time as they develop substantive arguments, often they will lose confidence in a good substantive argument simply because they haven't yet learned how to present it convincingly.

- Beware of internal inconsistencies in your argument methodology, even between two speakers on the one team e.g. if you appeal to plain meaning when it suits you and you or your team-mate refer to a purposive interpretation at other times, can you justify the differing recommendations? The same applies to strident criticisms about sloppy communications or drafting by the opposing party in the contractual communications. Vis Moot problems always have both parties behaving sub-optimally. People in glass houses should be careful of stone throwing. All self-serving arguments do not convince and this is just one example of that kind of argument.

6.4. Handling Questions

- If you present a fully structured and convincing case, you could in theory deflect every reasonable question. To do this you need to be aware of and address your weaknesses, e.g. "while Claimant will rely on . . . or while the Tribunal might think . . . etc., the better view is . . . because. . . ." A well structured argument along these lines will usually deflect questioning even from an interventionist arbitrator on your weakest points. This also goes back to the aim of being trustworthy and convincing. You want the listener to think they don't need to probe your argument as you will spoon-feed them with everything they need. They might not agree at the end but they know you will give them every idea they need.
- Nevertheless, a key part of preparation is preparation for questions. I aim through our weekly practice moots to ask everything possible within reason so students are not surprised and can prepare for all circumstances. (This is in fact the key pedagogical approach I take. I ask challenging questions throughout and all I ask is that students try their best to get an optimal argument for the benefit of their imaginary client. I don't expect them to have good answers until close to the end and my questions do aim to direct them to where the key ideas may emanate from.)
- Students are advised that you do one of three things with questions in a moot, either answer them well, or explain why the question is not necessary to your case theory or say you are unable to help and can you move on. The last option is the

last resort after your brain has collapsed under the weight of attempting the first two to the best of your ability! To that end, never be scared of silence. Silence in a moot should equal thinking time.

- Watch out for double barrelled questions e.g. some arbitrators will ask whether you agree with X (which seems something you have to agree with)? They will then say, if so, how can you argue Y? They usually are based on hypotheticals, seemingly unrelated to the facts of the problem. You want to pre-empt question 2 and answer it before it is asked if you can and certainly not trap yourself. It usually is wise to try and answer the first question in the negative or in a qualified manner as this usually defuses the trap.
- When you are being heavily questioned on an issue and want to move on, make sure you move from strength rather than weakness. This means having one more attempt at providing your answer in a positive fashion, hopefully in slightly different language or strategic direction. As you come to the end of your answer, indicate you have nothing further on this issue, that the Tribunal has enough to find in your favour on the point or via an alternative route and indicate that with the Tribunals permission, you wish to move on.

6.5. Presentation Tips

- In terms of "theatre" and body language, on the one hand you want to be as natural as possible but on the other, to be fully convincing and engaging, people who are gentler in persona usually have to try and get about 20% more animated while people who are seen as loud have to tone down by about 20%. (I tell students that this is also good practice for getting the balance right in job interviews!)
- Most people also do not modulate their voices enough. Changes of speed, emphasis and loudness as well as strategic pauses help keep peoples attention and also help you highlight your best points. On paper you can put words in bold or italics. When speaking, you have to emphasise with your voice.
- In terms of knowledge acquisition for moot arguments and questions, I explain to students that they need to be on top of a range of basics e.g. who has the burden on each issue, how

are words interpreted, where does good faith, common sense and commerciality fit in, how does a tribunal deal with inferences from known and unknown facts. These things are natural issues for experienced practitioners but are not taught well or in an integrated fashion in most law schools.

- Remember that you use sources to PERSUADE rather than as common law precedents. That means you don't cite authorities without explaining why this will help, e.g. you might suggest that a uniform view should be followed for the sake of consistency and because of the logic applied by the arbitrators/authors etc
- Remember, you are not responsible for weak facts or law in a moot or case, just for weak preparation and presentation.
- You need to find what type of advocacy notes work best for you. As short as possible that still gives you everything you need is the aim. As Respondent you must have space to make notes on Claimant arguments to fit in your general outline. (When students do practice moots in front of me they are never allowed to have more than one page in front of them and I will attack anything that sounds like a rote learned speech.)
- Judges usually do not tell you if they have not understood you. You need to judge by body language and their questions (e.g. where they ask a question that you have answered for the last 5 minutes) and retell the story if the penny has not dropped e.g. "if I can put it another way…").
- People often don't listen when they are tired, thinking about lunch or preparing to ask a question. You have to captivate their attention. You may need to get more animated mid-moot if you think they are wandering.

As I keep saying, if you put the effort in, you should get to a standard where you would not fear presenting your case before the most prestigious judges and against the most experienced and capable practitioners. It does take time and perseverance and improvements are not arithmetic and are often not discernible by the students involved. Most importantly, I tell students from beginning to end that I have no interest in competition results. I am only interested in their learning. Positive responses from the best arbitrators at the moot are of course testament to their abilities but only the students and I can know what they were like when they started and the degree to which the process has helped them realise their abundant potential.

7. CONCLUSION

Understanding advocacy as persuasion, as a seamless exercise requiring a case strategy and developing that strategy in the context of the evidentiary approach of a particular tribunal, are key elements of effective practice for lawyers engaged in international arbitration. Firm based and university training to this end are each important initiatives that should be of the greatest benefit to budding practitioners.

Institutional Advocacy Training

At the 28 January 2010 ASA conference, training institutions and practitioners were invited to discuss various methods of advocacy training, such as teaching, traineeships, pupilage and arbitration moots.

Three such institutions, Swiss-based but with global reach, were represented. Their main features are summarised here.

SAA – SWISS ARBITRATION ACADEMY[1]

Location:	Zurich, Switzerland
Type of Institution:	SAA is a private Swiss institution organised as a corporation under the Swiss Code of Obligations (SAA AG). The purpose of the corporation is the operation of a private academy for continuing legal education in international arbitration. Staempfli Verlag AG is one of the original and major shareholders. The Board of Directors of the SAA consists of three members of the Academic Council and of two representatives of Staempfli Verlag AG.
Faculty:	Arbitration practitioners from Switzerland and elsewhere
Training for:	Young practicing lawyers.
Format:	Four modules of one week each. The modules are: Fundamentals of International arbitration; How to commence arbitration proceedings; Taking of Evidence, hearings, discovery, interim measures; and From the Hearing to the Challenge and Enforcement of the Award. In order to accommodate working professionals, each week starts on a Thursday and ends on a Monday night.
Specific Advocacy Training:	Three of the four modules are in the form of mock arbitrations. The participants take part in practical exercises.

1 www.swiss-arbitration-academy.ch.

FIAA – FOUNDATION FOR INTERNATIONAL ARBITRATION ADVOCACY[2]

Location: Geneva, Switzerland, but workshops can take place in different locations (see below)

Type of Institution: FIAA is a Swiss foundation with charitable and educational purposes. FIAA's stated purposes are:

a. "to promote effective and ethical advocacy skills and techniques in international arbitration;
b. to provide training in effective and ethical advocacy skills and techniques for international arbitration;
c. to analyze, develop and implement methods of training in effective and ethical advocacy skills and techniques for international arbitration;
d. to provide a forum for arbitrators, counsel and academics to analyze, develop and promote effective and ethical advocacy and dispute resolution skills and techniques for international arbitration; and
e. to ensure links between academia and practising lawyers for the purpose of developing know-how and standards for international arbitration."

Training for: Arbitration practitioners. FIAA also runs the International Advocacy Workshop for students in the Geneva MIDS (see next page).

Faculty: Advocacy instructors and international arbitration practitioners.

Format: Three-day workshops, twice a year in different locations. FIAA provides specialised workshops on the questioning of fact witnesses in international arbitration.

Specific Advocacy Training: Advocacy training is the purpose of FIAA, which has been established to meet "the compelling need for high quality advocacy training specifically designed for international arbitration".

---

2 www.fiaa.com.

MIDS – GENEVA LL.M. IN INTERNATIONAL DISPUTE SETTLEMENT[3]

Location: Geneva, Switzerland

Type of Institution: MIDS is a common programme of the Graduate Institute for International and Development Studies (HEID) and of the Geneva University Law School.

Faculty: Professors of the Graduate Institute and Geneva University. Visiting professors and practitioners.

Training for: The MIDS is open to students having completed a first law degree.

Format: One academic year of full-time study in residence followed by two months of independent research and writing. The course is a mix of lectures, tutorials and workshops.

Specific Advocacy Training: Through a partnership with FIAA, MIDS students are offered a two-day workshop in witness examination in international arbitration.

---

3 www.mids.ch.

In-House Advocacy Training

In addition to dedicated advocacy-training institutions, certain law firms have in-house programmes to provide formal advocacy training to their associates. Two such firms contributed their approach to advocacy training at the 28 January 2010 ASA Conference.

HERBERT SMITH

OVERVIEW OF KEY ADVOCACY TRAINING MODULES FOR INTERNATIONAL ARBITRATION

In this short note, we have set out examples of certain advocacy training modules organised for international arbitration lawyers at Herbert Smith.

In addition—but not included here—are external programmes which associates are encouraged strongly to attend (such as those run by the Federation for International Arbitration Advocacy in Lausanne), and the numerous training sessions for advocacy in *litigation*, in which our arbitration associates also participate. In our London office, for example, all disputes associates (whether litigation or arbitration) are trained to become Solicitor Advocates (which consists, in part, of 5 days of training on evidence, procedure and ethics, followed by 4 days of advocacy training with a mock case study).

Of the arbitration-only sessions, the following examples illustrate the type of programme available. Ultimately, however, we consider that the best training is real, practical experience. As such, we always encourage associates to take responsibility for (at least part) of a hearing—whether on a specific point of law, or in relation to particular witnesses or experts—at the earliest possible stage in their career.

ANNUAL 2 DAY INTERNATIONAL ARBITRATION ADVOCACY WORKSHOP

This brings together arbitration associates from all of our offices, with a deliberate mix of common and civil law practitioners. Two full days are spent working through an arbitration case study, starting with refresher training on cross-examination and ending with a mock hearing. Video review is used, and each participant has a dedicated programme of individual feedback (as well as participating in broader, group sessions).

WITNESS HANDLING WORKSHOPS

We arrange a number of these each year, pitched at different levels of experience (from beginner through to refresher). One common feature of the programme is an explanation of differences in approach between domestic court procedure (wherever that court might be) and international arbitration.

REGULAR CROSS-EXAMINATION MASTERCLASSES

In addition to the witness handling workshops, regular masterclasses are arranged which focus exclusively on cross-examination (again, pitched at differing levels).

All of these sessions use simulation exercises (based on mock cases), and are invariably accompanied by video review. The Firm also uses a range of advocacy DVDs, which are used either as demonstrations or for critiquing.

WHITE & CASE LLP

White & Case educates its associates in arbitration advocacy through formal programs and training in preparation for hearings.

FORMAL ADVOCACY PROGRAMS

White & Case puts on a two-day formal arbitration advocacy program at least once per year. The location is rotated between Europe and the Americas. All arbitration associates are eligible to attend, but preference is given to those who are closest to the location and whom have not participated in the program in the past.

White & Case's program was designed by retired arbitration partner Rayner Hamilton and Trial Advocacy Professor James Seckinger from the University of Notre Dame (U.S.), and has been improved over the years through the contributions of Paul Friedland and other arbitration partners. Faculty for the program are White & Case arbitration partners and counsel and outside advocacy professionals, including professors of courtroom advocacy and English barristers. A practicing international arbitrator, such as Charles Brower, is often invited as a guest lecturer to provide an additional perspective.

The associate participants in the program are divided into teams of three. Ideally, each team has one senior attorney, one mid-level and one junior person. The participants receive program materials at least six weeks in advance so that they have time to prepare. The materials consist of organization materials and schedules, advocacy guidelines and a mock record of witness statements and exhibits for a mock arbitration. One or two conference calls are held with the participants in advance of the program.

The program itself is divided into two segments. The first segment is a series of short lectures and practice sessions covering basic questioning techniques. This takes place on the first day of the program. The second day of the program is devoted to a mock arbitration using the materials that were provided in advance. The teams of three are paired off against one another. Each advocate has an opportunity to argue a motion/application, make opening and/or closing remarks and question witnesses on direct (limited), cross and redirect examinations. The advocates also play witnesses for each other. The faculty sit as arbitrators in panels of three and provide feedback as the day progresses and at the conclusion.

OTHER TRAINING – ARBITRATION HEARINGS

In preparing for arbitration hearings, White & Case associates are frequently paired with partners or senior associates to prepare witnesses and examinations for the hearing in question. If the associate appears capable and ready, the associate may be allowed to conduct the examination herself. While each arbitration is different, our experience is that White & Case tends to employ more attorneys as speaking advocates at hearings than our opponents.

APPENDICES

Association Suisse de l'Arbitrage
Schweiz. Vereinigung für Schiedsgerichtsbarkeit
Associazione Svizzera per l'Arbitrato
Swiss Arbitration Association

The ASA CHARTER of Advocacy in International Commercial Arbitration

As a constituent part of international commerce, international commercial arbitration must be at the service of the international business community. This implies that the principal objective of international commercial arbitration must be the efficiency of the process, avoiding unnecessary confrontation, producing fair and equitable results and contributing to the restoration of constructive business relations.

The arbitral process must be tailored to meet the needs and legitimate expectations of the users, namely the parties. The parties' representatives, referred to here as "Counsel", have a key role to play in this process. First of all, Counsel owe loyalty and effective services to their clients. However, the ASA Charter considers the role of Counsel in its entirety, which encompasses all of the required skills that Counsel need to master in order to ensure that the international commercial arbitration process is responsive to the needs and expectations of its constituency. It is these skills that form effective advocacy in international commercial arbitration and that the ASA Charter seeks to promote.

ASA is aware that these objectives can be promoted in a variety of ways. Therefore the present Charter sets out some basic principles. As experience in the application of the Charter advances, these principles may evolve and may be refined.

1. COUNSEL AND THE ARBITRAL TRIBUNAL

Effective advocacy in international commercial arbitration is above all communication with the tribunal, understanding its task and assisting the tribunal in meeting its obligations. This implies the following:

- Making a clear, concise and user-friendly presentation of the case, setting out the position of the party represented by

Counsel and identifying those aspects in which this position differs from that of the opponent(s);

- ensuring that all submissions, whether written or oral, are logically structured and as succinct as possible;
- presenting the evidence in a manner which facilitates the task of the tribunal in establishing the facts that are relevant for its decision;
- assisting the tribunal in understanding the legal and technical rules relevant for the resolution of the dispute;
- ensuring that evidence and argument on legal and technical matters are not presented in a misleading manner; and
- assisting the tribunal in understanding the cultural, commercial and technical context in which the client and other protagonists conduct their business and the perspective in which they perceive the case.

In preparing and presenting the case, Counsel should be mindful that the arbitral tribunal must reach a decision without the support of outside assistance; user-friendly presentation of the material is desirable.

Further, it should be borne in mind that the procedure is not assisted by Counsel entering into long, protracted, argumentative and non-constructive correspondence with the other side and most importantly, with the arbitral tribunal. Such tactics prove to be costly and are contrary to the principal objective of international commercial arbitration, which is to provide users with an efficient instrument for the resolution of international disputes.

2. COUNSEL AND THE ARBITRAL PROCEDURE

Most counsel in international commercial arbitration have received their training and initial experience in or by reference to some form of domestic litigation. When approaching international arbitration proceedings, Counsel should be mindful that the training and experience of other players in the process may differ, having regard to various legal, social and cultural backgrounds.

Whilst the rules and practices in domestic civil procedure may have features which are useful also for international arbitration, Counsel should not be concerned with the exportation of these rules and practices into the international arena but rather, with the efficiency in presenting the parties' cases, thereby avoiding unnecessary cost and delay. It is important to bear in mind that each case has its own specificity and needs, and as such, Counsel should cooperate with the arbitral tribunal in ensuring that the needs of the case are best met by the procedure

The purpose of the procedure is to resolve the dispute and not to settle personal scores between the protagonists. Counsel should contribute to a sober and business-like approach to the procedure.

Cooperation with the tribunal and opposite counsel in the organisation of the procedure is desirable, for it promotes the efficient conduct of the arbitration and assists in concentrating the time and energy of all the participants on the substantive resolution of the dispute.

In some cases, "ambush" tactics may create short-term advantages, but ultimately resort to such methods neither assists the arbitral tribunal nor contributes to the sound administration of justice, which requires that both parties have a fair chance to be heard. Such manoeuvres cause a loss of time and money, not to mention the ill feelings created by a sense of unfairness which normally would attach to an ambush. Therefore, they do not even serve the interests of the lawyer's client.

3. COUNSEL AND THE OTHER PLAYERS IN THE ARBITRAL PROCESS

An arbitral tribunal normally approaches the case from the assumption that the parties to the dispute have legitimate reasons to differ in their positions. Effective advocacy respects this basic assumption. Consequently,

- the dignity of the other party, its witnesses and experts should be respected; they should be treated with courtesy;
- personal attacks should be avoided; and
- allowance should be made for difficulties in communication due to differences in language or cultural background.

4. COUNSEL AND THE CLIENT PARTY TO THE ARBITRATION

It is Counsel's principal task to convey to the tribunal the client's perspective of the dispute forcefully and convincingly.

In order to do this effectively, Counsel should seek to promote a realistic assessment of the case and its possible outcome with the client. This will require: a critical analysis of the client's views and positions;

pointing out strength and weaknesses of the case to the client; and associating the client closely in the development of strategic options. Counsel must continuously update the assessment of the strengths and weaknesses in the client's case as the case progresses. This ensures that the case strategy is properly monitored at all times.

The in-depth and continuous assessment of the strengths and weaknesses of the client's case also enables Counsel to advise the client on opportunities for settlement. This is an important task of Counsel, for it serves the ultimate purpose of the process: the rapid and cost-efficient resolution of disputes.

A major function of Counsel's role is to assemble the evidence that is to be presented to the arbitral tribunal. Counsel should perform this task with critical objectivity, developing the case theory based on the evidence that is available, rather then bending the evidence to meet a case theory that has been preconceived by the client or created to meet its expectations.

Efficiency in preparing and conducting the case may require mobilisation of the client's in-house resources. Counsel should be open to this potential but, at the same time should keep the strategic control over the process.

If other services are required, such as technical experts, accountants or claims consultants, it is Counsel's obligation to see to it that their contribution addresses the points in issue and assists the tribunal.

Counsel must be mindful of the cultural and commercial context of the client. One of the principal tasks of Counsel consists in assisting the tribunal in understanding this context.

In all cases, Counsel must retain the requisite independence from the client and avoid any uncritical personal espousal of the client's position. Although this is one of the most difficult tasks for Counsel, it is of paramount importance and constitutes one of the most effective hallmarks of effective advocacy in international commercial arbitration.

6 February 2009

Association Suisse de l'Arbitrage
Schweiz. Vereinigung für Schiedsgerichtsbarkeit
Associazione Svizzera per l'Arbitrato
Swiss Arbitration Association

The ASA PRIZE for Advocacy in International Commercial Arbitration

EXPLANATORY NOTE

With the objective of promoting the effective resolution of international commercial disputes through arbitration, the Swiss Arbitration Association (ASA) offers a prize at regular intervals for Counsel who, through their exceptional talents in advocacy, contribute most effectively to this objective. As an organization with wide-ranging international membership, including arbitrators, counsel and users with extensive international arbitration practice, ASA sees itself as ideally placed to contribute to this objective by identifying and publicizing good examples of advocacy in international arbitration. It plans to announce the first Laureate at ASA's annual conference on 29 January 2010 in Geneva.

ASA has set out in the "ASA CHARTER of Advocacy in International Commercial Arbitration" the principles of advocacy which it seeks to promote, thereby identifying the criteria for the choice of the laureate. The Charter is not cast in stone and will be developed with the experience gained in the administration of the Prize.

Any member of the international arbitration community may propose candidates for the prize. However, a member of a law firm or other organization may not propose another member of the same organization. The proposal must identify the candidate and provide basic personal information including a succinct statement (no longer than one page) setting out the reasons why the candidate is considered suitable for the prize. Concrete examples illustrating the candidate's advocacy are desirable and may be attached to the proposal in a form guaranteeing confidentiality. Personal references are also welcome.

The prize is not restricted to ASA members, nor are there any other restrictions on eligibility, except that ASA Executive Board members are not eligible. The laureate may be an established or an up and coming practitioner. In all cases, the candidate's performance in the spirit of the ASA CHARTER will be the decisive factor in selecting the laureate.

Proposals should be submitted to the ASA Executive Board. The author of the proposal must disclose his or her identity when submitting the proposal but the ASA Executive Board shall treat the proposal confidentially and the name of the proposing person shall not be made public.

The ASA Executive Board will set up a Selection Committee of three members, elected for a renewable term of 3 years. The election of new members or the re-election of sitting members will take into account the need for renewal, whilst at the same time guaranteeing an appropriate degree of continuity. Also, the ASA Executive Board will ensure that the composition of the Selection Committee will draw from a variety of legal, cultural and professional backgrounds and can extend the membership to persons invited in their individual capacity or nominated by an organization such as ACCE.

The Selection Committee will scrutinize the proposals with the objective of selecting five candidates for the prize (the Shortlist). It may add further candidates to the selection process and may conduct its own enquiries. For this purpose, the Selection Committee members may contact the references indicated in the proposal or any other person who may provide information about the advocacy skills of the candidate. The Selection Committee shall ensure that the enquiry process and any information obtained shall remain confidential.

For each of the five candidates the Selection Committee will prepare a file containing the reasoned proposal and other information on the candidate, including reports on recent actual performance. The file will contain an explanation by the Selection Committee as to why it considers the candidate to be suitable for the prize.

The ASA Executive Board will consider the files of the candidates on the Shortlist prepared by the Selection Committee. After deliberation the ASA Executive Board will decide on the laureate by secret ballot.

The laureate will be invited to the Annual ASA Conference and presented to the participants. The *laudatio* will be held by a member of the ASA Executive Board determined by that board. The laureate will receive recognition as "ASA Laureate in International Arbitration Advocacy" and her or his name will be so identified on the ASA Website, together with the *laudatio*.

August 2009

Attachment: The ASA Charter of Advocacy in International Commercial Arbitration
Form for the Proposal of a Candidate

Winner of the 2010 ASA Prize for Advocacy in International Commercial Arbitration

Wilmer Cutler Pickering Hale and Dorr
LLP 4 Carlton Gardens Pall Mall, London
SW1Y 5AA England Tel: +44 (207) 871 1000
Fax: +44 (207) 839 3537
franz.schwarz@wilmerhale.com

Franz T. Schwarz is a partner of Wilmer Cutler Pickering Hale and Dorr LLP in London. He specializes in international arbitration and dispute resolution and is Vice-Chair of the Firm's International Arbitration Group.

PRACTICE

Mr. Schwarz focuses on complex multi-jurisdictional disputes. He has extensive experience with arbitral practice, procedure and advocacy both in civil and common law systems.

Mr. Schwarz regularly serves as arbitrator, including as chairman of arbitral tribunals, and is included on the roster of several major arbitral institutions. He has represented clients in over sixty arbitrations, both in ad hoc proceedings and before all major arbitral institutions (including ICC, LCIA, Vienna, and Stockholm), at various seats (including London, Paris, Rome, Vienna, Geneva, Zurich, The Hague, Lausanne, and Stockholm) and under a wide variety of applicable laws. Mr. Schwarz has particular experience with contractual and corporate disputes in the telecommunications, energy, finance, media, and trade sectors.

Additionally, Mr. Schwarz counsels clients on conflict of laws issues and international enforcement of arbitration awards and judgments, including against state entities, and frequently advises parties on the protection of foreign investments under bilateral investment treaties and similar instruments.

PROFESSIONAL ACTIVITIES

Mr. Schwarz lectures international arbitration at Zurich University, the Vienna School of Economics, and Johns Hopkins in Bologna. He is a Member of the Chartered Institute of Arbitrators, the IBA Arbitration Sub-Committee on the New York Convention, the LCIA, DIS and the Swiss and Austrian Arbitration Associations. Mr. Schwarz participates in the LCIA working committee to represent the LCIA at the sessions of the UNCITRAL Working Group II on the reform of the model rules in international commercial arbitration.

From 2003-2007, Mr. Schwarz served on the Executive Board of the ICDR's Young & International Arbitration program, which he co-founded. He is the recipient of the American Arbitration Association's Distinguished Service Award "for his distinguished service and support of international arbitration and mediation."

QUALIFICATIONS

Mr. Schwarz is an Austrian *Rechtsanwalt* and member of the Vienna bar. He graduated as *Magister Juris* from University of Vienna School of Law, Austria (1995, top of class) and has obtained an LL.M. degree from the London School of Economics (with merits).

PUBLICATIONS

Mr. Schwarz frequently speaks and publishes on topical issues of international arbitration. Recent publications include:

Commentary on the International Rules of the American Arbitration Association, in: Weigand (ed.), Practitioner's Handbook on International Arbitration (2nd ed. Oxford University Press, March 2010)

Das Verfahren vor dem Schiedsgericht (ZPO §§ 594-602), in: Handbuch des Österreichischen Schiedsrechts, Rechberger /Oberhammer/Liebscher (Hrsg), (Springer Verlag, 2010)

The Limits of Party Autonomy in International Arbitration, in: International Arbitration Forum Vienna, (Eleven International Publishing, December 2009)

Arbitration in: Austria — Legal Changes and Trends, in: The European and Middle Eastern Arbitration Review, Global Arbitration Review (2009) The Vienna Rules --A Commentary on International Commercial Arbitration in Austria, (Kluwer Law International, January 2009)

The Procedural Order Public and The Internationalization of Public Order In Arbitration, Austrian Arbitration Yearbook 2008, Manz (2008)

The New Vienna Rules, Arbitration International Vol 23 No 4 (2007)

Enforcing Foreign Arbitral Awards in England, Tagungsband DIS, Dresden 2007 Arbitration in Germany, International Comparative Legal Guide to International Arbitration, Global Legal Group (2007, with Hanno Wehland)

ASA Conference
29 January 2010

Hôtel Président Wilson, Geneva
47 Quai Wilson | 1201 Geneva

Advocacy in International Commercial Arbitration

09:00 - 09:10	WELCOME ADDRESS AND INTRODUCTION TO THE CONFERENCE TOPIC	Michael E. Schneider, President ASA; LALIVE, Geneva
09:10 - 09:30	INTRODUCTION: WHY ADVOCATES? - WHAT ADVOCATES? - THE ROLE OF COUNSEL IN INTERNATIONAL ARBITRATION	Peter J. Turner, Freshfields Bruckhaus Deringer, Paris
09:30 - 10:30	PANEL 1 THE ROLE AND DESIRED QUALITIES OF COUNSEL AS SEEN FROM THE PERSPECTIVE OF THE PLAYERS IN THE PROCESS Corporate counsel, arbitrators and lawyers discuss their experiences with advocates in international arbitration, their expectations of good advocacy in a critical analysis of The ASA Charter of Advocacy in International Commercial Arbitration Issues discussed will include: – differences in culture and style – evolution of the role model over time – the relationship with the client and the tribunal – the relationship with witnesses and experts – the use of consultants and their management DISCUSSION Panel and Floor	Bruce Gailey, Chief Litigation Counsel for Alstom's Power Sector, Baden Prof. Gabrielle Kaufmann-Kohler, Lévy Kaufmann-Kohler, Geneva Martin Burkhardt, Lenz & Staehelin, Zurich Michael Young, Herbert Smith, Paris **Moderator**: Elliott Geisinger, Vice-president ASA, Schellenberg Wittmer, Geneva

10:30 – 11:00	COFFEE BREAK	
11:00 – 12:00	CONTINUATION OF PANEL 1	
12:00 – 12:30	ASA PRIZE FOR ADVOCACY IN INTERNATIONAL COMMERCIAL ARBITRATION – Award to laureate – Laudatio	
12:30 – 14:00	LUNCH	
14:00 – 15:30	**PANEL 2** **RULES AND SANCTIONS** – How are the rules identified: conflict of laws or transnational standards? – Relevant substantive rules, e.g. privilege, confidentiality obligations and reporting obligations, lawyer's testimony, role in document production and use of evidence of dubious origin – Possible sanctions: exclusion from the hearing and the case, decisions on costs – Publicity, reporting and rating – "transparency", levelling the playing ground or unfair competition DISCUSSION Panel and Floor	Georges-Albert Dal, Dal & Valdekens, Brussels Matthew Gearing, Allen & Overy, Hong Kong **Moderator**: Michael E. Schneider
15:30 – 16:00	COFFEE BREAK	

16:00 - 17:30	**PANEL 3** **ADVOCACY TRAINING** Some training institutions and practitioners will discuss various methods and approaches such as teaching, traineeships, pupilage and moot tribunal proceedings **DISCUSSION PANEL 3** Panel and Floor	Prof. Daniel Girsberger, Faculty of Law, Lucerne David Roney, Schellenberg Wittmer, Geneva Prof. Thomas Schultz, Law Faculty of Law, Geneva Prof. Jeff Waincymer, Faculty of Law, Monash University in Melbourne/Australia **Moderator**: Elliott Geisinger
17:30 - 17:45	**CLOSING ADDRESS**	**Michael E. Schneider**

SELECTIVE BIBLIOGRAPHY

Advocacy is a regular research subject. This bibliography is by no means intended to fully cover the subject but may provide indications to interested readers.

G.-D.-E. Adair, A.-L. Shah, *On Trial: Advocacy Skills Law and Practice,* Toronto, Ont. [etc.]: Butterworths, 1992.

P. Bergman, *Trial Advocacy in a Nutshell,* St Paul, MI: West, 2nd Edition, 1989.

D. Bishop, E.-G. Kehoe, *The Art of Advocacy in International Arbitration,* 2nd Edition, Juris Publishing, May 2010.

J.-W. Cooley, S. Lubet, *Arbitration Advocacy,* NITA Practical Guide Series, 2nd Edition, 2003.

M. Hill, A.-V. Sinicropi, A.-L. Evenson, *Winning Arbitration Advocacy,* Bureau of National Affairs, 1997.

L. Gratiot, C. Mécary *et al*, *Art et technique de la plaidoirie d'aujourd'hui,* Paris:Lexis-Nexis, 2011.

H.-W. Kritzer, *Legal Advocacy – Lawyers and Non-Lawyers at Work,* The University of Michigan Press, 1998.

P. Murphy, *Evidence and Advocacy,* London Blackstone, 3rd Edition, 1990.

R.-K. Soonavala, M.-C. Chagla, *Advocacy: Its Principles and Practice: Dealing With the Art of Advocacy, Examination-in-Chief ...* [etc.], Bombay: Tripathi, 1960.

A. Scalia, B.-A. Garner, "Making your case: The Art of Persuading Judges", Thomson West Law, September 2009.

R.-C. Waites, *Courtroom psychology and trial advocacy,* ALM Publishing, 2003.

*   *

T. Arnold, "Advocacy in Mediation", *Worldwide Forum on the Arbitration of Intellectual Property Disputes : Jointly organized by the World Intellectual Property Organization (WIPO) and the American Arbitration Association (AAA),* Geneva, March, 3 and 4, 1994, Geneva: WIPO, pp. 277-291.

Ch.-D. Blach, "The Art of War and the Art of Trial Advocacy: Is There A Common Ground?", *Mercer Law Review,* vol. 42, pp. 861-873.

D.-J. Bederman, "Tibor Várady's Advocacy before the International Court of Justice", *Resolving International Conflicts: Liber amicorum Tibor Várady,* Budapest [etc]: Central European University Press, 2009, pp. 21-44.

J. Beechey, "Advocacy in International Commercial Arbitration: England", *The Art of Advocacy in International Arbitration,* Huntington, NY: Juris, 2004, pp. 233-258.

G. Binder, "Representing Nazism: Advocacy and Identity at the Trial of Klaus Barbie", *Yale Law Journal,* vol. 98 (1999), pp. 1321-1383.

D. Bishop, "Advocacy in International Commercial Arbitration: United States", *The Art of Advocacy in International Arbitration,* Huntington, NY: Juris, 2004, pp. 309-353.

D. Bishop, "Advocacy from the Arbitrator's Perspective", *The Art of Advocacy in International Arbitration,* Huntington, NY: Juris, 2004, pp. 441-447.

D. Bishop, "Toward a Harmonized Approach to Advocacy in International Arbitration" *The Art of Advocacy in International Arbitration,* Huntington, NY: Juris, 2004, pp. 451-490.

D. Bishop, A. P. Schiffer, "Effective Advocacy in International Arbitration", *The Metropolitan Corporate Counsel,* May 2005, p. 25.

C. Bogert, "Human Rights Advocacy in Global Governance: A Case Study of Human Rights Watch in *The New Dynamics of Multilateralism: Diplomacy, International Organizations and Global Governance,* Boulder, CO: Westview Press, (2010), pp. 169-182.

D.-J.-A. Cairns, "Advocacy and the Functions of Lawyers in International Arbitration", *Liber Amicorum Bernado Cremades,* Madrid La Ley, 2010, pp. 291-307.

J.-R. Crawford, "Advocacy before the International Court of Justice and Other International Tribunals in State-to-State Cases", *The Art of Advocacy in International Arbitration,* Huntington, NY: Juris, 2004, pp. 11-38.

H.-A. Cull, D.-W. Allen, "Human Rights Advocacy in the Philippines: Report on a Mission to the Philippines August 1985 on Behalf of the International Commission of Jurists", CIJ, 1987.

Y. Derains, "The International Chamber of Commerce - Continuing Education of Lawyers and Arbitrators", *Yearbook Commercial Arbitration,* vol. V, pp. 301 – 304.

Y. Derains, "Training: a Challenge for the Future of International Arbitration - Editorial", Journal of International Arbitration, vol 5- 3, pp. 5-8.

D. Flader, "Comment on Jan Paulsson's essay: 'Cultural Differences in Advocacy in International Arbitration'", *Transnational Dispute Management*, December 2010.

E. Gaillard, Ph. Pinsolle, "Advocacy in International Commercial Arbitration: France", *The Art of Advocacy in International Arbitration*, Huntington, NY: Juris, 2004, pp. 133-150.

T. Giovaninni, "The Continental European Perspective and Practice of Advocacy" D. Bishop, E.-G. Kehoe, *The Art of Advocacy in International Arbitration*, 2nd Edition, Juris Publishing, 2010, pp. 499 ff.

D.-R. Haigh, B. Beck, "Advocacy in International Commercial Arbitration: Singapore", *The Art of Advocacy in International Arbitration*, Huntington, NY: Juris, 2004, pp. 259-307.

K. Hobér, "Advocacy in International Commercial Arbitration: Sweden", *The Art of Advocacy in International Arbitration*, Huntington, NY: Juris, 2004, pp. 169-194.

M. Hunter, "Ethics of the International Arbitrator", *Arbitration*, 1987, pp. 219- 220.

M. Hunter, "Reflections on Advocacy and the Art of Persuasion", *The Litigator*, p. 275 [1995].

M. Hwang, "Advocacy in International Commercial Arbitration: Singapore", *The Art of Advocacy in International Arbitration*, Huntington, NY: Juris, 2004, pp. 413-437.

P.-A. Jordan, "Criminal Defense Advocacy in Russia under the 2001 Criminal Procedure Code", *The American Journal of Comparative Law*, 2005, vol. 53-1, pp. 157-187.

D.-W. Layton, J.-O. Miranda, « Advocacy before the World Trade Organization Dispute Settlement Panels in Trade Remedy Cases », *The Art of Advocacy in International Arbitration*, Huntington, NY: Juris, 2004, pp. 75-129.

J.-L. Loftis, "Advocacy of Private Disputes Before International Claims Resolution Bodies" *The Art of Advocacy in International Arbitration*, Huntington, NY: Juris, 2004, pp. 39-74.

C.-M. Loperena Ruiz, "Advocacy in International Commercial Arbitration: Mexico" *The Art of Advocacy in International Arbitration*, Huntington, NY: Juris, 2004, pp. 399-412.

J.-P. Manno, "Advocacy and Diplomacy: NGOs and the Great Lakes Water Quality Agreement" in *Environmental NGOs in World Politics: Linking the Local and the Global*, 1994, pp. 69-120.

P. Miljeteig-Olssen, "Advocacy of Children's Rights: The Convention As More Than a Legal Document?", *Human Rights Quarterly: A Comparative and International Journal of the Social Sciences, Philosophy, and Law*, vol. 12, pp. 148-155.

J. Paulsson, "Standards of Conduct for Counsel in International Arbitration", *Essays in Honour of H. Smit*, 3 *The American Review of International Arbitration* 214 (1992).

J. Paulsson, "Cultural Differences in Advocacy in International Arbitration", *Transnational Dispute Management*, 1er December 2010.

I. Quintana, A. Fortún, "Advocacy in International Commercial Arbitration: Spain" in *The Art of Advocacy in International Arbitration*, Huntington, NY: Juris, 2004, pp. 151-168.

C.-A. Rogers, "Fit and Function in Legal Ethics: Developing a Code of Conduct for International Arbitration", 23 *Michigan Journal of International Law* 241 (2002).

C.-A. Rogers, "Context and Institutional Structure in Attorney Regulation: Constructing an Enforcement Regime for International Arbitration", 39 *Stamford Journal of International Law* 1 (2003).

C.-A. Rogers, "Regulating International Arbitrators: A Functional Approach to Developing Standards of Conduct", *Transnational Dispute Management*, 1st December 2010.

S.-J. Siggelakis, "Advocacy on Trial", *The American Journal of Legal History: Official Publication of the American Society for Legal History*, Vol. 36, pp. 499-516.

Ch.-R. Stevens, "Foreign Lawyer Advocacy in International Arbitration in Japan", *Arbitration International*, Vol. 13 (1997) No. 1, pp. 103-104.

G.-S. Tawil, "Advocacy in International Commercial Arbitration: Argentina", *The Art of Advocacy in International Arbitration*, Huntington, NY: Juris, 2004, pp. 355-398.

J. Toulmin, "A Worldwide Common Code of Professional Ethics?", *Fordham International Law Journal,* vol. 15 (1991-1992), pp. 673-675.

P.-Y. Tschanz, "Advocacy in International Commercial Arbitration: Switzerland", *The Art of Advocacy in International Arbitration,* Huntington, NY: Juris, 2004, pp. 195-232.

M. Schieber, "There is no such thing as a free a question: examining the hidden costs of trial advocacy", *Mercer Law Review,* 1991, vol. 42, pp. 847-860.

Seth Center, "Supranational Public Diplomacy: The Evolution of the UN Department of Public Information and the Rise of Third World Advocacy", *The United States public diplomacy: new directions in cultural and international history,* Leiden [etc]: Nijhoff, 2010, pp. 135-163.

H. Smit, "The Future of International Commercial Arbitration: A Single Transnational Institution?", *Colum. J. Transnat' L.* 9, vol. 25 (1986), p. 22.

G. S. Tawil, "Advocacy in International Commercial Arbitration: Argentina", *The Art of Advocacy in International Arbitration,* Huntington, NY: Juris, 2004.

N.-C. Ulmer, "Ethics and Effectiveness: Doing Well by Doing Good", *The Commercial Way to Justice: The 1996 International Conference of the Chartered Institute of Arbitrators,* 167-171.

Detlev F. Vagts, "The International Legal Profession: A Need for More Governance?", *American Journal of International Law,* vol. 90 (1996), p. 250.

Detlev F. Vagts, "International Legal Ethics and Professional Responsibility", *American Soc. Int'l L. Proc.* vol. 92 (1998), pp. 378-379.

V.-V. Veeder, "2001 Goff Lecture: The lawyers' duty to arbitrate in good faith", *Arbitration International,* vol. 18 (2002), pp. 431-435.

INDEX

Q

R

S

T